Yankee Doodle Boy

Joseph Plumb Martin

Yankee Doodle Boy

*A Young Soldier's Adventures in
the American Revolution
Told by Himself*

Edited by George F. Scheer

With Maps & Illustrations by
Victor Mays

Holiday House/New York
1995

The Company of Military Historians through its Reviewing Board takes pride in sponsoring this book as a popular, responsible work in military history.

This book was originally published by William R. Scott, Inc. in 1964.

Library of Congress Cataloging-in-Publication Data
Martin, Joseph Plumb, 1760–1850.
[Narrative of some of the adventures, dangers, and sufferings of a
Revolutionary soldier]
Yankee Doodle boy : a young soldier's adventures in the American
Revolution / told by himself ; edited by George F. Scheer ; with
maps & illustrations by Victor Mays.
p.   cm.
Previously published: New York : W.R. Scott, c1964.
Simplified version of: Private Yankee Doodle, 1962.
Includes index.
ISBN 0-8234-1176-1
ISBN 0-8234-1180-X (pbk.)
1. Martin, Joseph Plumb, 1760–1850
2. United States—History—Revolution, 1775–1783—Personal
narratives. [1. Martin, Joseph Plumb, 1760–1850.
2. United States-History—Revolution, 1775–1783
—Personal narratives.] I. Scheer, George F. II. Mays, Victor,
1927–   ill. III. Title.
E275.M38   1995   94-34227   CIP   AC
973.3′8—dc20
[B]

For my son

GEORGE F. SCHEER III

so that he and his generation may better understand and cherish the liberty won for them by men like Joseph Plumb Martin and his comrades-in-arms.

Table of Contents

Editor's Foreword

On a warm July night in 1776, a fifteen-year-old Connecticut farm boy, big and husky for his age, went to town with some of his friends and enlisted in the Continental Army. Joseph Martin had been thinking about it a long time, ever since fighting had broken out more than a year before at Lexington and at Concord and the American Revolution had begun. At first, he had been too young to join the army, and his grandfather, with whom he lived, had objected. And he himself had had some misgivings about a long term of service. But when the army called for volunteers for six months only, he decided to try a short hitch. He signed enlistment papers (indentures he called them) in his home town of Milford and set off to serve for six months. Before he was through with the war, he had served seven long years.

He fought at the battles of Long Island, White Plains, Germantown, Monmouth, Fort Mifflin, and others. He hutted at Morristown in the worst winter of the entire eighteenth century, and he encamped on the bleak hills of Valley Forge. He made the great march from the Hudson River to Yorktown, he stormed the fortifications of Cornwallis, and he watched the British Army lay down its arms in surrender. He served nearly two more years before he put aside musket, knapsack and canteen to take up hoe, hammer and saw as a farmer and a carpenter.

Joseph Martin never forgot the hard times of the American Revolution: the fright, pain and death of battle; the vermin and sickness of camp and hospital; the grinding agony of marches up and down the country without rest or sleep, half-naked and barefoot. All his long life he remembered the cold and the misery of winter camps; the days of ' belly-twisting hunger; and the nights of lonely, perilous sentry duty. But he also remembered the other things: the companionship of the men with whom he lived and went to battle; the pranks and games and sports frolicking soldiers enjoyed together; the infrequent but deep pleasure of snug quarters and an occasional good meal; and the satisfactions of sticking to the job, of hard duty well done.

Soldiers often have pretty vague ideas about what they are fighting for, but Joseph Martin knew what his war was all about—freedom. That was his goal. That was his purpose. Through every hardship, when many Americans were willing to quit a dismal and discouraging war, he doggedly stood ground with the faithful and fought on. He was a youth who sensed the simple truth that a decent cause must and shall prevail, so long as men of belief stand for it without compromise and without fear.

Before the war and after, Joseph Martin lived the life of an ordinary citizen of his time. He was born on November 21, 1760, in western Massachusetts. Because his father, Ebenezer Martin, could not provide for all his children, Joseph, when seven, went to live with his grandfather near Milford. He never attended school, but somewhere he acquired an ability and a passion for reading and for self-expression.

When the war was over and Martin settled in Maine, he followed his grandfather's calling and became a farmer and carpenter. He built himself a house at the mouth of

Editor's Foreword

the lovely Penobscot River in a little community that came to be named Prospect. There, in 1794, he married eighteen-year-old Lucy Clewley and reared a family of several children.

In Prospect, Martin became a popular yarn-spinning veteran of the American Revolution. Finally, urged by his friends, he set down the whole story of his service in George Washington's Continental Army. In 1830, it was published under the title, *A Narrative of Some of the Adventures, Dangers and Sufferings of a Revolutionary Soldier, Interspersed with Anecdotes of Incidents That Occurred Within His Own Observation.* In 1962, it was my privilege to publish it again in a modern edition with a new title, *Private Yankee Doodle.* With the gracious permission of Little, Brown and Company, the publisher of *Private Yankee Doodle,* I have prepared this edition and called it *Yankee Doodle Boy.*

In this edition I have added at the beginning of each chapter an opening which I trust will aid the reader in identifying events and places to which Martin refers. I have omitted a number of Martin's passages and phrases that would be of little interest, and I have modernized his spelling. Where necessary I have broken up overly long paragraphs and repunctuated some sentences. However, Martin was a vivid and entertaining writer, whose words and syntax I have not presumed to change, even where an occasional sentence is involved or awkward. This is Joseph Martin's story the way he himself told it.

In his own defense, Martin made a proud statement. The grammarian, he said, may find fault with his pages. He regretted he had not studied grammar "an hour" in his life, but, said he, "when I ought to have been doing that, I was forced to be studying the rules and articles of war. As to punctuation, my narrative is in the same predicament as it is in respect to the other parts of grammar. I never learned the rules of punctuation any further than just to assist in fixing a comma to the British depredations in the state of New York; a semicolon in New Jersey; a colon in Pennsylvania; and a final period in Virginia."

There is no other book just like Joseph Martin's. Other Revolutionary War soldiers kept diaries and journals in which they recorded the daily events of camp and field. But no other soldier, so far as historians know, wrote in so much valuable detail, with such robust good humor, and at such great length about the life of the private soldier of the Continental Army.

GEORGE F. SCHEER

Chapel Hill, North Carolina

Joseph Plumb Martin's

Narrative

I

War

Bells and alarm guns summon Joseph Martin from his grandfather's fields to Milford. The village is astir with the news: British soldiers and Massachusetts colonists have fired on each other at Lexington and at Concord. The American Revolution has begun. Milford men march off to aid their countrymen at Boston and at New York, but fourteen-year-old Joseph is too young to enlist.

The heroes of all Adventures have, or are supposed to have, ancestors, or some root from which they sprang. I shall not undertake to trace my pedigree, but just observe that my father was the son of a "substantial New England farmer," as we Yankees say, in the state of Connecticut and county of Windham.

My mother was likewise a "farmer's daughter"; her native place was in the county of New Haven, in the same state.

After my father left [Yale] college, he studied divinity, had "a call," accepted it, and was settled in the county of Berkshire in the Commonwealth of Massachusetts as a gospel minister of the Congregational order; in which county of Berkshire I, the hero of this Narrative, first made my appearance in this crooked, fretful world, upon the twenty-first day of November, in the year 1760.

I lived with my parents until I was upwards of seven years old, when I went to live with [my] good old grandsire; for good he was, particularly to me. He was wealthy and I had everything that was necessary for life. It is true my grandsire kept me pretty busily employed, but he was kind to me in every respect, always gave me a playday when convenient, and was indulgent to me almost to a fault.

I remember the stir in the country occasioned by the Stamp Act, but I was so young that I did not understand the meaning of it. I likewise remember the disturbances that followed the repeal of the Stamp Act, until the destruction of the tea at Boston and elsewhere. I was then thirteen or fourteen years old and began to understand something of the works going on. I used, about this time, to inquire a deal about the French [and Indian] War, which had not been long ended. My grandsire would talk with me about it while working in the fields. I thought then, nothing should induce me to get caught in the toils of an army.

Time passed smoothly with me till the year 1774 arrived. The smell of war began to be pretty strong, but I was determined to have no hand in it. I felt myself to be a real coward. What—venture my carcass where bullets fly! That will never do for me. Stay at home out of harm's way, thought I. But the pinch of the game had not arrived yet. I had seen nothing of war affairs and consequently was but a poor judge in such matters.

War

The winter passed off without any very frightening alarms, and the spring of 1775 arrived. Expectation of some fatal event seemed to fill the minds of most of the considerate people throughout the country. I was plowing in the field about half a mile from home, about the twenty-first day of April, when all of a sudden the bells fell to ringing and three guns were repeatedly fired in succession down in the village. What the cause was we could not conjecture. I had some fearful forebodings. The [British] regulars are coming in good earnest, thought I. My grandsire immediately turned out the team and repaired homeward. I set off to see what the cause of the commotion was. I found most of the male people together. Soldiers for Boston were in requisition. A dollar deposited upon the drumhead was taken up by someone as soon as placed there, and the holder's name taken, and he enrolled with orders to equip himself as quick as possible. My spirits began to revive at the sight of the money offered. The seeds of courage began to sprout. O, thought I, if I were but old enough to put myself forward, I would be the possessor of one dollar, the dangers of war to the contrary notwithstanding.

The men that had engaged "to go to war" went as far as the next town, where they received orders to return, as there was a sufficiency of men already engaged, so that I should have had but a short campaign had I gone.

This year there were troops raised both for Boston

17

and New York. Some from the back towns were billeted at my grandsire's. Their company and conversation began to warm my courage to such a degree
that I resolved at all events to "go a sogering." Accordingly I used to pump my grandsire, in a round-
about manner, to know how he stood respecting it.
For a long time he appeared to take but little notice
of it. At length, one day, I pushed the matter so hard
upon him, he was compelled to give me a direct
answer, which was, that he should never give his
consent for me to go into the army unless I had the
previous consent of my parents. And now I was completely graveled; my parents were too far off to obtain their consent before it would be too late for the
present campaign. What was I to do? Why, I must
give up the idea, and that was hard; for I was as
earnest now to call myself and be called a soldier as
I had been a year before *not* to be called one. I
thought over many things and formed many plans,
but they all fell through, and I was forced to set
down and gnaw my fingernails in silence.

I said but little more about "soldiering" until the
troops raised in and near the town in which I resided
came to march off for New York. Then I felt bitterly
again. I accompanied them as far as the town line,
and it was hard parting with them then. Many of
my young associates were with them. My heart and
soul went with them, but my mortal part must stay
behind. By and by, they will come swaggering back,
thought I, and tell me of all their exploits, all their

"hair-breadth 'scapes," and poor Huff will not have a single sentence to advance.

The thoughts of the service still haunted me after the troops were gone, but what plan to form to get the consent of all, parents and grandparents, that I might procure the bewitching name of a soldier, I could not devise. Sometimes I thought I would enlist, let the consequences be what they would. Then again, I would think how kind my grandparents were to me, and ever had been, my grandsire in particular: I could not bear to hurt their feelings so much.

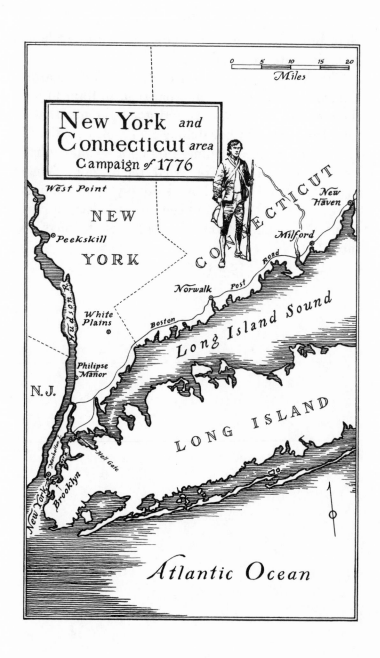

New York *and* Connecticut *area*
Campaign *of* 1776

0   5   10   15   20
Miles

West Point

NEW

Peekskill

YORK

CONNECTICUT

New
Haven

Milford

Norwalk

Post Road

White
Plains

Boston

Philipse
Manor

N.J.

Long Island Sound

Hudson R.

New York

Manhattan I.

Hell Gate

Brooklyn

LONG ISLAND

Jo

Atlantic Ocean

II

The Campaign of 1776

Joseph Martin, now fifteen, enlists for six months in the Continental Army and goes to New York, where General George Washington is preparing to meet a massive British assault from the sea. He fights at Long Island, Kip's Bay and Harlem Heights. When the British drive Washington northward out of New York, he fights again at White Plains. He escorts sick soldiers to Connecticut to "recruit" or to restore their health and strength. He is lectured sharply by a Tory lady, and he happily receives his discharge on Christmas Day.

During the winter of 1775-76, by hearing the conversation and disputes of the good old farmer politicians, I collected pretty correct ideas of the contest between this country and the mother country. I thought I was as warm a patriot as the best of them. The war was waged; we had joined issue, and it would not do to "put the hand to the plow and look back." I felt more anxious than ever to be called a defender of my country.

One evening, very early in the spring of this year, I chanced to overhear my grandma'am telling my grandsire that I had threatened to engage on board a man-of-war. I had told her that I would enter on

board a privateer then fitting out in our neighborhood. The good old lady thought it a man-of-war,
that and privateer being synonymous terms with her.
She said she could not bear the thought of my being
on board of a man-of-war. My grandsire told her
that he supposed I was resolved to go into the service in some way or other and he had rather I would
engage in the land service if I must engage in any.
This I thought to be a sort of consent for me to go,
and I determined to take advantage of it as quick as
possible.

Soldiers were at this time enlisting for a year's
service. I did not like that; it was too long a time for
me at the first trial. I wished only to take a priming
before I took upon me the whole coat of paint for a
soldier. However, the time soon arrived that gratified
all my wishes. In the month of June, orders came out
for enlisting men for six months from the twenty-
fifth of this month. The troops were styled new
levies. They were to go to New York. And notwithstanding I was told that the British army at that
place was reinforced by fifteen thousand men, it
made no alteration in my mind. I did not care if
there had been fifteen times fifteeen thousand, I
should have gone just as soon as if there had been
but fifteen hundred. I never spent a thought about
numbers. The Americans were invincible in my opinion. If anything affected me, it was a stronger desire
to see them.

I used frequently to go to the rendezvous, where
I saw many of my young associates enlist, had re-

peated banterings to engage with them, but still when it came "case in hand," I had my misgivings. If I once undertake, thought I, I must stick to it; there will be no receding.

But I one evening went off with a full determination to enlist at all hazards. When I arrived at the place of rendezvous I found a number of young men of my acquaintance there. The old bantering began.

"Come, if you will enlist, I will," says one.

"You have long been talking about it," says another. "Come, now is the time."

Thinks I to myself, I will not be laughed into it or out of it. I will act my own pleasure after all. But what did I come here for tonight? Why, to enlist. Then enlist I will. So seating myself at the table, enlisting orders were immediately presented to me. I took up the pen, loaded it with the fatal charge, made several mimic imitations of writing my name, but took especial care not to touch the paper with the·pen until an unlucky wight who was leaning over my shoulder gave my hand a stroke, which caused the pen to make a woeful scratch on the paper. "O, he has enlisted," said he. "He has made his mark; he is fast enough now." Well, thought I, I may as well go through with the business now as not. So I wrote my name fairly upon the indentures.

And now I was a *soldier*, in name at least, if not in practice; but I had now to go home, after performing this, my heroic action. How shall I be received there? But the report of my adventure had reached there before I did. In the morning when I first saw

23

my grandparents, I felt considerably sheepish. The old gentleman first accosted me with, "Well, you are going a soldiering then, are you?" I had nothing to answer. I would much rather he had not asked me the question. I saw that the circumstance hurt him and the old lady, too; but it was too late now to repent. The old gentleman proceeded, "I suppose you must be fitted out for the expedition, since it is so." Accordingly, they did "fit me out" with arms and accouterments, clothing, and cake, and cheese in plenty, not forgetting to put my pocket Bible into my knapsack. Good old people! They wished me well, soul and body. I sincerely thank them for their kindness and love to me, from the first time I came to live with them to the last parting hour.

I was now what I had long wished to be, a soldier. I had obtained my heart's desire; it was now my business to prove myself equal to my profession. Well, to be short, I went with several others of the company on board a sloop bound to New York; had a pleasant passage; passed through the strait called Hell Gate, where all who had not before passed it had to pay a treat; arrived at New York; marched up into the city, and joined the rest of the regiment that were already there.

I was called out every morning at reveille beating, which was at daybreak, to go to our regimental parade in Broad Street, and there practice the manual exercise. I was brought to an allowance of provisions which, while we lay in New York, was not bad. If there was any deficiency it could in some measure be

24

supplied by procuring some kind of sauce, but I began soon to miss grandsire's table. However, I reconciled myself as well as I could; it was my own seeking. I had had no compulsion.

I remained in New York two or three months, when, sometime in the latter part of the month of August, I was ordered upon a fatigue party. We had scarcely reached the grand parade when I saw our sergeant major directing his course up Broadway, towards us, in rather an unusual step for him. He soon arrived and informed us and then the commanding officer of the party that he had orders to take off all belonging to our regiment and march us to our quarters, as the regiment was ordered to Long Island, the British having landed in force there. Although this was not unexpected to me, yet it gave me rather a disagreeable feeling, as I was pretty well assured I should have to snuff a little gunpowder. However, I went to my quarters, packed up my clothes, and got myself in readiness for the expedition as soon as possible. I then went to the top of the house where I had a full view of that part of the Island. I distinctly saw the smoke of the field artillery, but the distance and the unfavorableness of the wind prevented my hearing their report, at least but faintly. The horrors of battle then presented themselves to my mind in all their hideousness. I must come to it now, thought I. Well, I will endeavor to do my duty as well as I am able and leave the event with Providence. We were soon ordered to our regimental parade, from which, we were marched off for the ferry.

The Campaign of 1776

At the lower end of the street were placed several casks of sea bread, made, I believe, of cinnamon and peas-meal, nearly hard enough for musket flints. The casks were unheaded and each man was allowed to take as many as he could as he marched by. As my good luck would have it, there was a momentary halt. I improved the opportunity thus offered me, as every good soldier should upon all important occasions, to get as many of the biscuits as I possibly could. No one said anything to me and I filled my bosom and took as many as I could hold in my hand, a dozen or more in all, and when we arrived at the ferry stairs I stowed them away in my knapsack. We quickly embarked on board the boats. As each boat started, three cheers were given by those on board, which was returned by the numerous spectators who thronged the wharves. They all wished us good luck, apparently; although it was with most of them perhaps nothing more than ceremony.

We soon landed at Brooklyn, upon the Island, marched up from the ferry to the plain. We now began to meet the wounded men, another sight I was unacquainted with, some with broken arms, some with broken legs, and some with broken heads. The sight of these a little daunted me, and made me think of home, but the sight and thought vanished together. We marched a short distance, when we halted to refresh ourselves. Whether we had any other victuals besides the hard bread I do not remember, but I remember gnawing at them. They were hard enough to break the teeth of a rat. One of the soldiers complaining of thirst to his officer—"Look at that man," said he, pointing to me; "he is not thirsty, I will warrant it." I felt a little elevated to be styled a *man*.

While resting here, which was not more than twenty minutes or half an hour, the Americans and British were warmly engaged within sight of us.

We were soon called upon to fall in and proceed. We had not gone far, about half a mile, when we overtook a small party of the artillery dragging a heavy twelve-pounder upon a field carriage, sinking half-way to the naves in the sandy soil. They pled hard for some of us to assist them to get on their piece. Our officers, however, paid no attention to their entreaties, but pressed forward towards a creek, where a large party of Americans and British were engaged. By the time we arrived, the enemy had driven our men into the creek, or rather millpond, where such as could swim got across. Those that could not swim, and could not procure anything to buoy them up, sunk.

The British, having several fieldpieces stationed by a brick house, were pouring the canister and grapeshot upon the Americans like a shower of hail. They would doubtless have done them much more damage than they did, but for the twelve-pounder mentioned above; the men, having gotten it within sufficient distance to reach them, and opening a fire upon them, soon obliged them to shift their quarters.

There was in this action a regiment of Maryland troops, (volunteers) all young gentlemen. When they came out of the water and mud to us, looking like

28

water rats, it was a truly pitiful sight. Many of them were killed in the pond, and more were drowned. Some of us went into the water after the fall of the tide, and took out a number of corpses and a great many arms that were sunk in the pond and creek.

Our regiment lay on the ground we then occupied the following night. The next afternoon, we had a considerable tight scratch with about an equal number of the British. I do not recollect that we had any-one killed outright, but we had several severely wounded, and some, I believe, mortally.

Our regiment was alone upon a rising ground, cov-ered with a young growth of trees. We felled a fence of trees around us to prevent the approach of the ene-mies' horse. We lay there a day longer. In the latter part of the afternoon there fell a very heavy shower of rain which wet us all to the skin and much damaged our ammunition.

Just at dusk, I, with one or two others of our com-pany, went off to a barn, about half a mile distant, with intent to get some straw to lodge upon, the ground and leaves being drenched in water, and we as wet as they. I could not find any straw, but I found some wheat in the sheaf, standing by the side of the floor. I took a sheaf or two and returned as fast as I could to the regiment. When I arrived the men were all paraded to march off the ground. I left my wheat, seized my musket and fell into the ranks. We were strictly enjoined not to speak, or even cough, while on the march. All orders were given from officer to officer, and communicated to the men in whispers.

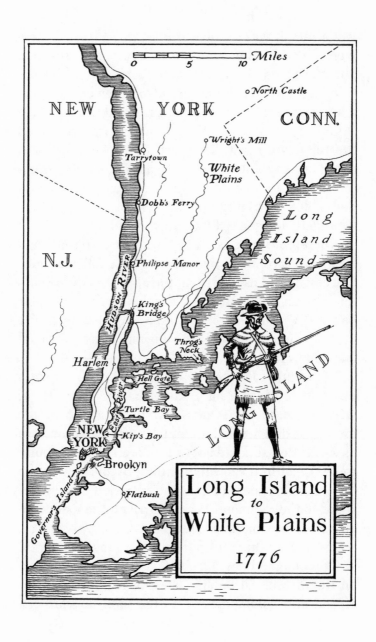

Miles

0 5 10

NEW YORK

CONN.

○ North Castle

○ Wright's Mill

Tarrytown

White Plains

Dobb's Ferry

N.J.

Long Island Sound

Philipse Manor

HUDSON RIVER

King's Bridge

Throg's Neck

Harlem

Hell Gate

East River

Turtle Bay

NEW YORK

Kip's Bay

LONG ISLAND

Brookyn

Governor's Island

Flatbush

Long Island
to
White Plains

1776

What such secrecy could mean we could not divine. We marched off in the same way that we had come on to the island, forming various conjectures among ourselves as to our destination. Some were of opinion that we were to endeavor to get on the flank, or in the rear of the enemy. Others, that we were going up the East River to attack them in that quarter; but none, it seems, knew the right of the matter. We marched on, however, until we arrived at the ferry, where we immediately embarked on board the bateaux and were conveyed safely to New York, where we were landed about three o'clock in the morning.

The next day the British showed themselves to be in possession of our works upon the island by firing upon some of our boats passing to and from Governors Island. Our regiment was employed during this day in throwing up a sort of breastwork at their alarm post upon the wharves facing the enemy, composed of spars and logs and filling the space between with the materials of which the wharves were composed—old broken junk bottles, flint stones, &c., which, had a cannon ball passed through, would have chanced to kill five men where the ball would one. But the enemy did not see fit to molest us.

We stayed several days longer in the city. One morning we discovered that a small [British] frigate had advanced up and was lying above Governors Island, close under the Long Island shore. Several other ships had come up and were lying just below the town. They seemed to portend evil. In the evening, just at dark, our regiment was ordered to

31

march to Turtle Bay, a place about four miles distant
on the East River, where were a large warehouse or
two, called then the King's stores, built for marine
stores belonging to the government before the war.

There was at this time about twenty-five hundred
barrels of flour in those storehouses, and it was conjectured that the frigate was to seize on this flour.
We were, therefore, ordered to secure it before the
British should have an opportunity to lay their un-
hallowed hands upon it. We arrived at the place
about midnight, and by sunrise or a little after had
secured the whole of it by rolling it up a steep bank
and piling it behind a ledge of rocks. While we were
employed in doing this, some other troops were constructing a small battery on a point of land opposite
the frigate (she having arrived during the night and
anchored just below us). As soon as we had finished
our work at the flour, the battery opened upon her
with two long twelve-pounders, which so galled her
ribs that her situation began to grow rather uneasy.
She never returned a shot at the battery, but got
underway as quick as possible and ran by us, there
being then a little wind. We all stood gazing at her
as she passed, when she sent us a nine-pound shot,
perhaps the best she had to send us, which passed
amongst us without injuring anyone. She ran a little
way up the river and came to anchor again.

We continued here some days to guard the flour.
We were forbidden by our officers to use any of it,
except our daily allowance. We used, however, to
purloin some of it to eat and exchange with the

inhabitants for milk, sauce, and such small matters as we could get for it.

One evening while lying here, we heard a heavy cannonade at the city, and before dark saw four of the enemy's ships that had passed the town and were coming up the East River. They anchored just below us. Half of our regiment was sent off under the command of our major to man something that were called "lines," although they were nothing more than a ditch dug along on the bank of the river with the dirt thrown out towards the water. They stayed in these lines during the night and returned to the camp in the morning unmolested.

The other half of the regiment went the next night under the command of the lieutenant colonel. We arrived at the lines about dark and were ordered to leave our packs in a copse wood under a guard and go into the lines without them. What was the cause of this piece of *wise* policy I never knew, but I knew the effects of it, which was that I never saw my knapsack from that day to this, nor did any of the rest of our party unless they came across them by accident in our retreat. We had a chain of sentinels quite up the river, for four or five miles. At an interval of every half hour, they passed the watchword to each other, "All is well." I heard the British on board their shipping answer, "We will alter your tune before tomorrow night." And they were as good as their word for once.

It was quite a dark night, and at daybreak [September 15] the first thing that "saluted our eyes" was all the four ships at anchor with springs upon their cables and within musket shot of us. The *Phoenix* lying a little quartering and her stern towards me, I could read her name as distinctly as though I had been directly under her stern. What is the meaning of all this, thought I, what is coming forward now? They appeared to be very busy on shipboard, but we lay still and showed our good breeding by not interfering with them, as they were strangers, and we knew not but they were bashful withal. As soon as it was fairly light, we saw their boats coming out of a creek or cove on the Long Island side of the water, filled with British soldiers. When they came to the edge of the tide, they formed their boats in line. They continued to augment their forces from the island until they appeared like a large clover field in full bloom. And now was coming on the famous Kip's Bay affair. I was there and will give a true statement of all that *I* saw during that day.

It was on a Sabbath morning. We lay very quiet in our ditch waiting their motions, till the sun was an hour or two high. We heard a cannonade at the city, but our attention was drawn toward our own guests. But they being a little dilatory in their operations, I stepped into an old warehouse which stood close by me with the door open inviting me in and sat down upon a stool. The floor was strewed with papers. I was very demurely perusing these papers when all of a sudden there came such a peal of thunder from the British shipping that I thought

my head would go with the sound. I made a frog's
leap for the ditch and lay as still as I possibly could
and began to consider which part of my carcass
was to go first. The British played their parts well;
indeed they had nothing to hinder them. We kept
the lines till they were almost leveled upon us, when
our officers, seeing we could make no resistance and
no orders coming from any superior officer and that
we must soon be entirely exposed to the rake of
their guns, gave the order to leave the lines.

In retreating we had to cross a level, clear spot
of ground forty or fifty rods wide, exposed to the
whole of the enemy's fire, and they gave it to us
in prime order. The grapeshot and langrage flew
merrily, which served to quicken our motions. When
I had gotten a little out of the reach of their combus-
tibles, I found myself with a neighbor of mine when
at home and one other man belonging to our regiment. Where the rest of them were I knew not.

We had not gone far before we saw a party of
men, apparently hurrying on in the same direction.
We endeavored hard to overtake them, but on approaching them we found that they were not of our
way of thinking: they were Hessians. We immediately altered our course and took the main road
leading to King's Bridge. We had not long been on
this road before we saw another party, just ahead
of us, whom we knew to be Americans. Just as we
overtook these, they were fired upon by a party of
British from a cornfield and all was immediately

in confusion again. I believe the enemy's party was small, but our people were all militia, and the demons of fear and disorder seemed to take full possession of all and everything on that day.

We had to advance slowly, for my comrade having been some time unwell was now so overcome by heat, hunger, and fatigue that he became suddenly and violently sick. I took his musket and endeavored to encourage him on. I was loath to leave him behind, although I was anxious to find the main part of the regiment if possible before night, for I thought that that part of it which was not in the lines was in a body somewhere. We soon came in sight of a large party of Americans ahead of us who appeared to have come into this road by some other route. We were within sight of them when they were fired upon by another party of the enemy. They returned but a very few shots and then scampered off as fast as their legs would carry them. When we came to the ground they had occupied, we found a wounded man and some of his comrades endeavoring to get him off. I stopped to assist them in constructing a sort of litter to lay him upon. My sick companion growing impatient moved on, and as soon as we had placed the wounded man upon the litter I followed.

While I was here, one or two of our regiment came up and we went on together. We had proceeded but a short distance, however, before we found our retreat cut off by a party of the enemy stretched across the island. I immediately quitted the road and went into the fields, where there happened to be a small spot of boggy land covered with low bushes and weeds. Into these I ran and squatting down concealed myself from their sight. Several of the British came so near to me that I could see the buttons on their clothes. They, however, soon withdrew and left the coast clear for me again. I then came out of my covert and went on, but what had become of my sick comrade or the rest of my companions I knew not. I still kept the sick man's musket. I was unwilling to leave it, for it was his own property and I knew he valued it highly and I had a great esteem for him. I had indeed enough to do to take care of my own concerns. It was exceeding hot weather, and I was faint, having slept but very little the preceding night, nor had I eaten a mouthful of victuals for more than twenty-four hours.

I waddled on as well and as fast as I could, and soon passed across the corner of one field and through a gap in a cross fence into another. Here I found a number of men resting under the trees and bushes in the fences. Almost the first I saw was my sick friend. I was exceeding glad to find him, for I had but little hope of ever seeing him again. He was sitting near the fence with his head between his knees. I tapped him upon the shoulder and asked him to get up and go on with me. "No," said he, at the same time regarding me with a most pitiful look, "I must die here." I endeavored to argue the case with him, but all to no purpose; he insisted

upon dying there. I told him he should not die there
nor anywhere else that day, if I could help it, and
at length with more persuasion and some force I
succeeded in getting him upon his feet again and
moving on.

We went on a little distance when we overtook
another man belonging to our company. He had
just been refreshing himself with some bread and
dry salt fish and was putting the fragments into his
knapsack. I longed for a bite, but I felt too bashful
to ask him and he was too thoughtless or stingy to
offer it. We still proceeded, but had not gone far
when we came up with the regiment, resting themselves on the cold ground after the fatigues of the
day. Our company all *appeared* to rejoice to see
us, thinking we were killed or prisoners. I was *sincerely* glad to see them, for I was once more among
friends or at least acquaintances. Several of the regiment were missing, among whom was our major. He
was a fine man and his loss was much regretted by
the men of the regiment. We were the last who came
up, all the others who were missing were either
killed or taken prisoners.

And here ends the Kip's Bay affair.

We lay that night upon the ground which the
regiment occupied when I came up with it. The
next day, in the forenoon, the enemy, as we expected, followed us "hard up" and were advancing
through a level field. Our Rangers and some few
other light troops were in waiting for them. Seeing
them advancing, the Rangers &c. concealed them-

selves in a deep gully overgrown with bushes. Upon the western verge of this defile was a post and rail fence, and over that, the afore-mentioned field. Our people let the enemy advance until they arrived at the fence, when they arose and poured in a volley upon them. How many of the enemy were killed and wounded could not be known, as the British were always as careful as Indians to conceal their losses. There were doubtless some killed, as I myself counted nineteen ball holes through a single rail of the fence at which the enemy were standing when the action began. The British gave back and our people advanced into the field. The action soon became warm.

Our regiment was now ordered into the field, and we arrived on the ground just as the retreating enemy were entering a thick wood. We soon came to action with them. The troops engaged, being reinforced by our regiment, kept them retreating until they found shelter under the cannon of some of their shipping lying in the North River.

We remained on the battleground [at Harlem Heights] till nearly sunset, expecting the enemy to attack us again, but they showed no such inclination that day. The men were very much fatigued and faint, having had nothing to eat for forty-eight hours; at least, the greater part were in this condition, and I among the rest. While standing on the field after the action had ceased, one of the men near the lieutenant colonel complained of being hungry. The colonel, putting his hand into his coat pocket,

40

took out a piece of an ear of Indian corn burnt as black as a coal. "Here," said he to the man complaining, "eat this and learn to be a soldier."

We now returned to camp. When we arrived, we found that our invalids, consisting of the sick, the lame, and the lazy, had obtained some fresh beef. Where the commissaries found the beef or the men found the commissaries in this time of confusion I know not, nor did I stop to ask. They were broiling the beef on small sticks in Indian style round blazing fires made of dry chestnut rails. The meat when cooked was as black as a coal on the outside and as raw on the inside as if it had not been near the fire. I asked no questions for conscience's sake, but fell to and helped myself to a feast of this raw beef, without bread or salt.

We had eight or ten of our regiment killed in the action and a number wounded, but none of them belonged to our company.

We remained here till sometime in the month of October without anything very material transpiring, excepting starvation and *that* had by this time become quite a secondary matter. Hard duty and nakedness were considered the prime evils, for the reader will recollect that we lost all our clothing in the Kip's Bay affair.

It now began to be cool weather, especially the nights. To have to lie as I did almost every night (for our duty required it) on the cold and often wet ground without a blanket and with nothing but thin summer clothing was tedious. I have often while

41

upon guard lain on one side until the upper side smarted with cold, then turned that side down to the place warmed by my body and let the other take its turn at smarting, while the one on the ground warmed, thus, alternately turning for four or six hours till called upon to go on sentry. And when relieved from a tour of two long hours at that business and returned to the guard again, [I] have had to go through the operation of freezing and thawing for four or six hours more. In the morning, the ground [often was] as white as snow with hoar frost. Or perhaps it would rain all night like a flood. All that could be done in that case was to lie down (if one could lie down), take our musket in our arms and place the lock between our thighs and "weather it out."

Sometime in October, the British landed at Throg's Neck, or Point, and by their motions seemed to threaten to cut off our retreat from [New] York Island. We were thereupon ordered to leave the island. We crossed King's Bridge and directed our course toward the White Plains. We saw parties of the enemy foraging in the country, but they were generally too alert for us. We encamped on the heights called Valentine's Hill, where we continued some days, keeping up the old system of starving. A sheep's head which I begged of the butchers who were killing some for the officers was all the provisions I had for two or three days.

We marched from Valentine's Hill for the White Plains in the night. There were but three of our men present. We had our cooking utensils (at that time the most useless things in the army) to carry in our hands. They were made of cast iron and consequently heavy. I was so beat out before morning with hunger and fatigue that I could hardly move one foot before the other. I told my messmates that I *could not* carry our kettle any further. They said they *would* not carry it any further. Of what use was it? They had nothing to cook and did not want anything to cook with. We were sitting down on the ascent of a hill when this discourse happened. We got up to proceed when I took up the kettle, which held nearly a common pailful. I could not carry it. My arms were almost dislocated. I sat it down in the road and one of the others gave it a shove with his foot and it rolled down against the fence, and that was the last I ever saw of it. When we got through the night's march, we found our mess was not the only one that was rid of their iron bondage.

We arrived at the White Plains just at dawn of day, tired and faint, encamped on the plains a few days and then removed to the hills in the rear of the plains. Nothing remarkable transpired while lying here for some time. One day after roll call, one of my messmates with me set off upon a little jaunt into the country to get some sauce of some kind or other.

When we arrived [back] at the camp, the troops were all parading. Upon inquiry we found that the British were advancing upon us. We packed up our things, which was easily done for we had but a trifle to pack, and fell into the ranks. Before we were ready to march, the battle had begun. Our regiment

then marched off, crossed a considerable stream of water which crosses the plain, and formed behind a stone wall in company with several other regiments and waited the approach of the enemy.

They were not far distant, at least that part of them with which we were quickly engaged. They were constructing a sort of bridge to convey their artillery &c. across the stream. They, however, soon made their appearance in our neighborhood. There was in our front, about ten rods distant, an orchard of apple trees. The ground on which the orchard stood was lower than the ground that we occupied but was level from our post to the verge of the orchard, when it fell off so abruptly that we could not see the lower parts of the trees. A party of Hessian troops and some English soon took possession of this ground. They would advance so far as just to show themselves above the rising ground, fire, and fall back and reload their muskets. Our chance upon them was, as soon as they showed themselves above the level ground, or when they fired, to aim at the flashes of their guns. Their position was as advantageous to them as a breastwork.

We were engaged in this manner for some time, when, finding ourselves flanked and in danger of being surrounded, we were compelled to make a hasty retreat from the stone wall. We lost, comparatively speaking, very few at the fence, but when forced to retreat we lost in killed and wounded a considerable number. One man who belonged to our company, when we marched from the parade, said,

"Now I am going out to the field to be killed," and he said more than once afterwards that he should be killed, and he was. He was shot dead on the field. I never saw a man so prepossessed with the idea of any mishap as he was. We fell back a little distance and made a stand, detached parties engaging in almost every direction.

We did not come in contact with the enemy again that day, and just at night we fell back to our encampment. In the course of the afternoon, the British took possession of a hill on the right of our encampment, which had in the early part of the day been occupied by some of the New York troops. This hill overlooked the one upon which we were and was not more than half or three fourths of a mile distant. The enemy had several pieces of field artillery upon this hill and, as might be expected, entertained us with their music all the evening. We entrenched ourselves where we now lay, expecting another attack. But the British were very civil, and indeed they generally were after they had received a check from Brother Jonathan for any of their rude actions.

During the night we remained in our new-made trenches, the ground of which was in many parts springy. In that part where I happened to be stationed, the water before morning was nearly over shoes, which caused many of us to take violent colds by being exposed upon the wet ground after a profuse perspiration. I was one who felt the effects of it and was the next day sent back to the baggage to get well again, if I could, for it was left to my own

exertions to do it and no other assistance was afforded me. I was not alone in misery; there were a
number in the same circumstances.

When I arrived at the baggage, which was not
more than a mile or two, I had the canopy of heaven
for my hospital and the ground for my hammock.
I found a spot where the dry leaves had collected
between the knolls. I made up a bed of these and
nestled in it, having no other friend present but the
sun to smile upon me. I had nothing to eat or drink,
not even water, and was unable to go after any myself, for I was sick indeed. In the evening, one of my
messmates found me and soon after brought me
some boiled hog's flesh and turnips, without either
bread or salt. I could not eat it, but I felt obliged to
him nothwithstanding.

The British, soon after this, left the White Plains
and passed the Hudson into New Jersey. We likewise
fell back [northward] to New Castle and Wright's
Mills. Here a number of our sick were sent off to
Norwalk in Connecticut to recruit. I was sent with
them as a nurse. We were billeted among the inhabitants. I had in my ward seven or eight *sick soldiers* who were (at least, soon after their arrival there)
as well in health as I was. All they wanted was a
cook and something for a cook to exercise his functions upon.

The inhabitants here were almost entirely Tories.
An old lady, of whom I often procured milk, used
to give me a lecture on my opposition to our good
King George. She always said that the regulars

would make us fly like pigeons. My patients would not use any of the milk I had of her for fear, as they said, of poison. I told them I was not afraid of her poisoning the milk; she had not wit enough to think of such a thing, nor resolution enough to do it if she did think of it.

Our surgeon came amongst us soon after this and packed us all off to camp, save two or three who were discharged. I arrived at camp with the rest, where we remained, moving from place to place as occasion required, undergoing hunger, cold, and fatigue until the twenty-fifth day of December, 1776, when I was discharged, my term of service having expired, at Philipse Manor in the state of New York near Hudson's River.

Here ends my first campaign. I learned something of a soldier's life, enough, I thought, to keep me at home for the future. Indeed, I was then fully determined to rest easy with the knowledge I had acquired in the affairs of the army. Accordingly, I sat off for my good old grandsire's, where I arrived, I think, on the twenty-seventh, two days after my discharge, and found my friends all alive and well. They appeared to be glad to see me, and I am sure I was *really* glad to see them.

III

The Campaign of 1777

Martin rejoins the army in April, after Washington's victories at Trenton and Princeton have turned the tide of American fortunes from despair to hope. He is inoculated for smallpox. He helps guard the Hudson Highlands against British invasion from Canada or New York. In October he fights at Germantown, where Washington vainly tries to recapture Philadelphia which the British had taken the week before. He serves at the defense of Fort Mifflin in the Delaware River, encamps for a time at Valley Forge, and settles down for the winter in the country with a foraging party.

The spring of 1777 arrived. I had begun to think again about the army. In the month of April, as the weather warmed, the young men began to enlist. Orders were out for enlisting men for three years, or during the war. The general opinion of the people was that the war would not continue three years longer. What reasons they had for making such conjectures I cannot imagine, but so it was. Perhaps it was their wish that it *might* be so, induced them to think that it *would* be so.

The inhabitants of the town were about this time put into what were called squads, according to

49

their ratable property. Of some of the most opulent, one formed a squad; of others, two or three, and of the lower sort of the people, several formed a squad. Each of these squads were to furnish a man for the army, either by hiring or by sending one of their own number.

I had an elbow relation, a sort of cousin-in-law, who had been in the army the two preceding campaigns, and now had a lieutenant's commission. One of the above-mentioned squads, wanting to procure a man, the lieutenant told them that he thought they might persuade me to go for them, and they accordingly attacked me, front, rear and flank. I thought, as I must go, I might as well endeavor to get as much for my skin as I could. Accordingly, I told them that I would go for them, and fixed upon a day when I would meet them and clinch the bargain. The day, which was a muster day of the militia of the town, arrived. I went to the parade, where all was liveliness, as it generally is upon such occasions, but poor *I* felt miserably. My execution day was come. I kept wandering about till the afternoon, among the crowd, when I saw the lieutenant, who went with me into a house where the men of the squad were, and there I put my name to enlisting indentures for the last time. And now I was hampered again. The men gave me what they agreed to. I forget the sum, perhaps enough to keep the blood circulating during the short space of time which I tarried at home after I had enlisted. They were now freed from any further trouble, at least for the present, and I had become the scapegoat for them.

Soon we had orders to assemble the regiment at Newtown, the residence of our colonel. Here we drew our arms and equipments. Uncle Sam was always careful to supply us with these articles, even if he could not give us anything to eat, drink, or wear. We stayed but a short time here, but went on to Danbury, where I had an ample opportunity to see the devastation caused there by the British. The town had been laid in ashes, a number of the inhabitants murdered and cast into their burning houses, because they presumed to defend their persons and property, or to be avenged on a cruel, vindictive invading enemy. I saw the inhabitants, after the fire was out, endeavoring to find the burnt bones of their relatives amongst the rubbish of their demolished houses. The streets, in many places, were literally flooded by the fat which ran from the piles of barrels of pork burnt by the enemy.

We stayed here but a short time, and then marched to Peekskill, on the Hudson River, and encamped in the edge of the Highlands, at a place called Old Orchard. I was soon ordered off, in company with about four hundred others of the Connecticut forces, to a set of old barracks, a mile or two distant in the Highlands, to be inoculated with the smallpox. We arrived at and cleaned out the barracks, and after two or three days received the infection, which was on the last day of May. We had a guard of Massachusetts troops to attend us.

The
MIDDLE COLONIES
Campaigns
of
1777-1781

NEW YORK

CONN.

Kingston

New Milford

Newburgh

West Point   Danbury

Ft. Montgomery   Ft Independence

Stony Pt.   Peekskill   Redding

King's Ferry   Verplanck's Pt.

Tappan   Bedford

Philipse Manor   White Plains

Dobbs Ferry

Morristown

Basking Ridge   NEW YORK

Springfield   LONG ISLAND

Bethlehem   Westfield   Elizabethtown

STATEN I.

PENNSYLVANIA

Princeton

Englishtown

Coryell's Ferry   Monmouth C.H.

Trenton

Bristol   Burlington

Valley Forge   Mt Holly

Lancaster   Haddonfield

PHILADELPHIA

Woodbury

Delaware R.

NEW JERSEY

Head of Elk

ATLANTIC

OCEAN

Annapolis

MD.   DEL.

MILES

0   25   50

Our hospital stores were deposited in a farmer's barn in the vicinity of our quarters.

I had the smallpox favorably as did the rest, generally. I left the hospital on the sixteenth day after I was inoculated, and soon after joined the regiment.

In the latter part of the month of June, or the beginning of July, I was ordered off in a detachment of about a hundred men, under the command of a captain, to the lines near King's Bridge, to join two regiments of New York troops which belonged to our brigade.

We arrived upon the lines and joined the other corps which was already there. No one who has never been upon such duty as those advanced parties have to perform can form any adequate idea of the trouble, fatigue and dangers which they have to encounter. Their whole time is spent in marches, especially night marches, watching, starving, and, in cold weather, freezing and sickness. If they get any chance to rest, it must be in the woods or fields, under the side of a fence, in an orchard or in any other place but a comfortable one, lying down on the cold and often wet ground, and, perhaps, before the eyes can be closed with a moment's sleep, alarmed and compelled to stand under arms an hour or two, or to receive an attack from the enemy; and when permitted again to endeavor to rest, called upon immediately to remove some four or five miles to seek some other place, to go through the same maneuvering as before. For it was dangerous to remain any length of time in one place for fear of being informed of by some Tory inhabitant (for there were a plenty of this sort of savage beast during the Revolutionary War) and ten thousand other causes to harass, fatigue and perplex.

We remained on this hard and fatiguing duty about six weeks. We marched to Peekskill and rejoined our regiments sometime in the fore part of the month of August. A short time after my arrival at Peekskill, I was sent off to King's Ferry, about five miles below, to take some bateaux that were there and carry them to Fort Montgomery, in the edge of the Highlands.

While upon this tour of duty, an accident happened which caused me much trouble and pain. After we had arrived at the fort with the boats, we tarried an hour or two to rest ourselves, after which we were ordered to take a couple of the boats and return again to King's Ferry. Wishing to be the first in the boat, I ran down the wharf and jumped into it. There happened to be the butt part of an oar lying on the bottom of the boat, and my right foot, on which the whole weight of my body bore, alighted directly upon it. It rolled over and turned my foot almost up to my ankle, so that my foot lay nearly in a right angle with my leg. I had then to go to the ferry, where I was landed, and having no acquaintance with any of the party, most of whom were New Yorkers and no great friends to the Yankees, I was obliged to hop on one foot all the way, upwards of five miles, not being able in the whole

distance to procure a stick to assist me, although I
often hobbled to the fences on each side of the road
in hopes to obtain one. It was dark when I was
landed at the ferry, and it was quite late before I
arrived at the camp. Some of my messmates went
immediately for the surgeon, but he was at a game
of backgammon and could not attend to minor affairs. However, in about an hour he arrived, bathed
my foot, which was swelled like a bladder, fumbled
about it for some time, when he gave it a wrench,

which made me, like the old woman's dying cat,
"merely yawl out."

The next day, as I was sitting under the shade
before my tent, my foot lying upon a bench, swelled
like a puffball, my captain passed by and must needs
have a peep at it. I indulged his curiosity, upon
which he said it was not set right, and taking hold
of it, he gave it a twist, which put it nearly in the
same condition it was at first. I had then to send for
Mr. Surgeon again, but he was not to be found.
There was a corporal in our company who professed
to act the surgeon in such cases, and he undertook
the job and accomplished it, but it was attended
with more difficulty than the first time, and with
more pain to me. It was a long time before it got
well and strong again, indeed it never has been entirely so well as it was before the accident. I was
not long confined by it, however, but was soon able
to perform my duty in the army again.

Our troops, not long after this, marched to join
the main army in Pennsylvania. The heavy baggage
was left to come on after them, and I, being an in-
valid, was left as one of the guard to conduct it. The
baggage soon followed the troops, and I underwent
not a little trouble on the march in consequence of
my lame foot. When I joined the regiment the baggage was immediately sent back to Bethlehem,
nearly fifty miles in the country, and I was again
sent with it as a guard. I was resolved not to stay at
Bethlehem, and as soon as we arrived there I con-
trived to get the permission of the officers of the

guard to return to camp immediately. I arrived at camp the second day after leaving the baggage.

When I arrived at camp it was just dark, the troops were all preparing for a march. Early in the evening we marched in the direction of Philadelphia. We naturally concluded there was something serious in the wind. We marched slowly all night. In the morning there was a low vapor lying on the land which made it very difficult to distinguish objects at any considerable distance.

About daybreak our advanced guard and the British outposts came in contact [near Germantown]. The curs began to bark first and then the bulldogs. Our brigade moved off to the right into the fields. We saw a body of the enemy drawn up behind a rail fence on our right flank. We immediately formed in line and advanced upon them. Our orders were not to fire till we could see the buttons upon their clothes, but they were so coy that they would not give us an opportunity to be so curious, for they hid their clothes in fire and smoke before we had either time or leisure to examine their buttons. They soon fell back and we advanced, when the action became general. The enemy were driven quite through their camp. They left their kettles, in which they were cooking their breakfasts, on the fires, and some of their garments were lying on the ground, which the owners had not time to put on.

Affairs went on well for some time. The enemy were retreating before us, until the first [American] division that was engaged had expended their ammunition. Some of the men unadvisedly calling out that their ammunition was spent, the enemy were so near that they overheard them. They first made a stand and then returned upon our people, who, for want of ammunition and reinforcements, were obliged in their turn to retreat, which ultimately resulted in the rout of the whole army.

There were several other circumstances which contributed to the defeat of our army on that day, but as I am narrating my own adventures, and not a history of the war, I shall omit them.

I had now to travel the rest of the day, after marching all the day and night before and fighting all the morning. I had eaten nothing since the noon of the preceding day, nor did I eat a morsel till the forenoon of the next day, and I needed rest as much as victuals. I could have procured that if I had had time to seek it, but victuals was not to be found.

After the army had collected again and recovered from their panic, we were kept marching and countermarching, starving and freezing, nothing else happening, although that was enough, until we encamped at a place called the White Marsh, about twelve miles to the northward of Philadelphia. While we lay here, there was a spell of soft still weather, there not being wind enough for several days to dispel the smoke caused by the fires in camp. My eyes were so affected by it that I was not able to open them for hours together. The ground, which was soft and loamy, was converted into mortar, and so dirty was it, that any hogsty was preferable to our

58

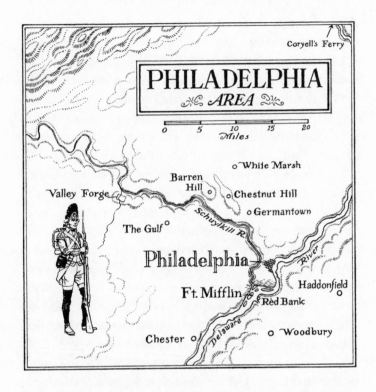

The following labels appear on the map:

PHILADELPHIA *AREA*

Coryell's Ferry

0 5 10 15 20
Miles

White Marsh
Barren Hill
Chestnut Hill
Valley Forge
Germantown
Schuylkill R.
The Gulf
River
Philadelphia
Haddonfield
Ft. Mifflin
Red Bank
Chester
Delaware
Woodbury

tents to sleep in; and to cap the climax of our misery, we had nothing to eat, nor scarcely anything to wear.

Soon our two Connecticut regiments were ordered off to defend the forts on the Delaware River, below the city [of Philadelphia].

We arrived at Woodbury, New Jersey, which was the end of our present journey. We encamped near the village, planted our artillery in the road at each end of it, placed our guards and prepared to go into Fort Mifflin which was then besieged by the British. Here I endured hardships sufficient to kill half a dozen horses. In the cold month of November, without provisions, without clothing, not a scrap of either shoes or stockings to my feet or legs, and in this condition to endure a siege in such a place as that, was appalling in the highest degree.

The island, as it is called, is nothing more than a mud flat in the Delaware, lying upon the west side of the channel. It is diked around the fort, with sluices so constructed that the fort can be laid under water at pleasure. On the eastern side, next the main river, was a zig-zag wall of hewn stone, built, as I was informed, before the Revolution at the king's cost. At the southeastern part of the fortification was a battery of several long eighteen-pounders. At the southwestern angle was another battery with four or five twelve- and eighteen-pounders and one thirty-two-pounder. At the northwestern corner was another small battery with three twelve-pounders. There were also three blockhouses in different parts of the enclosure, but no cannon mounted upon them, nor were they of any use whatever to us while I was there. On the western side, between the batteries, was a high embankment, within which was a tier of palisadoes. In front of the stone wall, for about half its length, was another embankment, with palisadoes on the inside of it, and a narrow ditch between them and the stone wall. On the western side of the fortification was a row of barracks, extending from the northern part of the works to about half the length of the fort. On the northern end was another block of barracks which reached nearly across the fort from east to west. In front of these was a large square two-story house, for the accommodation of the officers of the garrison. Neither this house nor the barracks were of much use at this time, for it was as much as a man's life was worth to enter them, the enemy often directing their shot at them in particular.

In front of the barracks and other necessary places were parades and walks; the rest of the ground was soft mud. I have seen the enemy's shells fall upon it and sink so low that their report could not be heard when they burst, and I could only feel a tremulous motion of the earth at the time. At other times, when they burst near the surface of the ground, they would throw the mud fifty feet in the air.

The British had erected five batteries with six heavy guns in each and a bomb battery with three long mortars in it on the opposite side of the water, which separated the island from the main on the west, and which was but a short distance across. They had also a battery of six guns a little higher up the river, at a place called the Hospital Point.

Our batteries were nothing more than old spars and timber laid up in parallel lines and filled between with mud and dirt. The British batteries in the course of the day would nearly level our works, and we were, like the beaver, obliged to repair our dams in the night. During the whole night, at intervals of a quarter or half an hour, the enemy would let off all their pieces. Although we had sentinels to watch them and at every flash of their guns to cry, "a shot," upon hearing which everyone endeavored to take care of himself, yet they would ever and anon, in spite of all our precautions, cut up some of us.

The engineer in the fort was a French officer by the name of [François Louis de] Fleury. He was a very austere man and kept us constantly employed day and night. There was no chance of escaping from his vigilance.

Between the stone wall and the palisadoes was a kind of yard or pen, at the southern end of which was a narrow entrance not more than eight or ten feet wide, with a ditch about four feet wide in the middle, extending the whole length of the pen. Here, on the eastern side of the wall, was the only place in the fort that anyone could be in any degree of safety. Into this place we used to gather the splinters broken off the palisadoes by the enemy's shot and make a little fire, just enough to keep from suffering. We would watch an opportunity to escape from the vigilance of Colonel Fleury, and run into this place for a minute or two's respite from fatigue and cold.

When the engineer found that the workmen began to grow scarce, he would come to the entrance and call us out. He had always his cane in his hand, and woe betided him he could get a stroke at. At his approach I always jumped over the ditch and ran down on the other side, so that he could not reach me, but he often noticed me and as often threatened me, but threatening was all. He could never get a stroke at me, and I cared but little for his threats.

It was utterly impossible to lie down to get any rest or sleep on account of the mud, if the enemy's shot would have suffered us to do so. Sometimes some of the men, when overcome with fatigue and want of sleep, would slip away into the barracks to catch a nap, but it seldom happened that they all came out again alive. I was in this place a fortnight and can say in sincerity that I never lay down to sleep a minute in all that time.

The British knew the situation of the place as well as we did. And as their point-blank shot would not reach us behind the wall, they would throw elevated grapeshot from their mortar. When the sentries had cried, "a shot," and the soldiers, seeing no shot arrive, had become careless, the grapeshot would come down like a shower of hail about our ears.

We had a thirty-two-pound cannon in the fort, but had not a single shot for it. The British also had one in their battery upon the Hospital Point, which raked the fort, or rather it was so fixed as to rake the parade in front of the barracks, the only place we could pass up and down the fort. The artillery officers offered a gill of rum for each shot fired from that piece, which the soldiers would procure. I have seen from twenty to fifty men standing on the parade waiting with impatience the coming of the shot, which would often be seized before its motion had fully ceased and conveyed off to our gun to be sent back again to its former owners. When the lucky fellow who had caught it had swallowed his rum, he would return to wait for another, exulting that he had been more lucky or more dexterous than his fellows.

What little provisions we had was cooked by the

invalids in our camp and brought to the island in
old flour barrels. It was mostly corned beef and hard
bread, but it was not much trouble to cook or fetch
what we had.

We continued here, suffering cold, hunger and
other miseries, till the fourteenth day of November.
On that day, at dawn, we discovered six ships of the
line, all sixty-fours, a frigate of thirty-six guns, and a
galley in a line just below the *chevaux-de-frise;* a
twenty-four-gun ship (being an old ship cut down),
her guns said to be all brass twenty-four-pounders,
and a sloop of six guns in company with her, both
within pistol shot of the fort, on the western side. We
immediately opened our batteries upon them, but

they appeared to take very little notice of us. We heated some shot, but by mistake twenty-four-pound shot were heated instead of eighteen, which was the caliber of the guns in that part of the fort. The enemy soon began firing upon us and there was music indeed. The soldiers were all ordered to take their posts at the palisadoes, which they were ordered to defend to the last extremity, as it was expected the British would land under the fire of their cannon and attempt to storm the fort.

Some of our officers endeavored to ascertain how many guns were fired in a minute by the enemy, but it was impossible. The fire was incessant. In the height of the cannonade it was desirable to hoist a signal flag for some of our galleys that were lying above us to come down to our assistance. The officers inquired who would undertake it. As none appeared willing for some time, I was about to offer my services. I considered it no more exposure of my life than it was to remain where I was. The flagstaff was of easy ascent, being an old ship's mast, having shrouds to the ground, and the round top still remaining. While I was hesitating, a sergeant of the artillery offered himself. He accordingly ascended to the round top, pulled down the flag to affix the signal flag to the halyard, upon which the enemy, thinking we had struck, ceased firing in every direction and cheered. "Up with the flag!" was the cry of our officers in every part of the fort. The flags were accordingly hoisted, and the firing was immediately renewed.

The sergeant then came down and had not gone

half a rod from the foot of the staff when he was cut in two by a cannon shot. This caused me some serious reflections at the time. He was killed! Had I been at the same business I might have been killed, but it might have been otherwise ordered by Divine Providence, we might have both lived. The enemy's shot cut us up. I saw five artillerists belonging to one gun cut down by a single shot. And I saw men who were stooping to be protected by the works, but not stooping low enough, split like fish to be broiled.

About the middle of the day some of our galleys and floating batteries, with a frigate, fell down [the river] and engaged the British with their long guns, which in some measure took off the enemy's fire from the fort. The cannonade continued without interruption on the side of the British throughout the day. Nearly every gun in the fort was silenced by midday. Our men were cut up like cornstalks. I do not know the exact number of the killed and wounded but can say it was not small, considering the numbers in the fort, which were only the able part of the Fourth and Eighth Connecticut regiments, with a company or two of artillery, perhaps less than five hundred in all.

As soon as it was dark we began to make preparations for evacuating the fort and endeavoring to escape to the Jersey shore. When the firing had in some measure subsided and I could look about me, I found the fort a picture of desolation. The whole area was as completely plowed as a field. The buildings of every kind [were] hanging in broken fragments, and the guns all dismounted, and how many of the garrison sent to the world of spirits, I knew not. If ever destruction was complete, it was here. The surviving part of the garrison were now drawn off and such of the stores as could conveniently be taken away were carried to the Jersey shore.

I happened to be left with a party of seventy or eighty men to destroy and burn all that was left in the place. After the troops had left the fort and were embarking at the wharf, I went to the waterside to find one of my messmates to whom I had lent my canteen in the morning. I found him lying in a long line of dead men who had been brought out of the fort to be conveyed to the mainland to have the last honors conferred upon them. Poor young man! He was the most intimate associate I had in the army, but he was gone, with many more as deserving as himself.

I returned directly back into the fort to my party and proceeded to set fire to everything that would burn, and then repaired immediately to the wharf where three bateaux were waiting to convey us across the river. And now came another trial. Before we could embark the buildings in the fort were completely in flames, and they threw such a light upon the water that we were as plainly seen by the British as though it had been broad day. Almost their whole fire was directed at us. Sometimes our boat seemed to be almost thrown out of the water, and at length a shot took the sternpost out of the rear boat. We had then to stop and take the men from the crippled boat into the other two, and now the shot and water flew merrily. But by the assistance of a kind Providence we escaped without any further injury and landed, a little after midnight, on the Jersey shore.

We marched a little back into some pitch-pine woods, where we found the rest of the troops that had arrived before us. They had made up some comfortable fires and were enjoying the warmth, and that was all the comfort they had to partake of, except rest, for victuals was out of the question. I wrapped myself up in my blanket and lay down upon the leaves and soon fell asleep and continued so till past noon, when I awoke from the first sound sleep I had had for a fortnight. Indeed, I had not laid down in all that time. The little sleep I had obtained was in cat naps, sitting up and leaning against the wall, and I thought myself fortunate if I could do that much. When I awoke I was as crazy as a goose shot through the head.

We left our flag flying when we left the island, and the enemy did not take possession of the fort till late in the morning after we left it.

We now prepared to leave Red Bank. I was ordered on a baggage guard. It was not disagreeable to me as I had a chance to ride in a wagon a considerable part of the night. We went in advance of the troops, which made it much easier getting along. We had been encouraged during the whole siege with the promise of relief. "Stand it out a little longer and we shall be relieved," had been the constant cry. The second day of our march we met two regiments advancing to relieve us. When asked where they were going, they said to relieve the garrison in the fort. We informed them that the British had done that already!

Our guard passed through Haddonfield in the night. We arrived early in the morning at a pretty village called Mount Holly. Here we waited for the troops to come up.

We marched from hence and crossed the Delaware again between Burlington and Bristol. Here we procured a day's ration of southern salt pork (three fourths of a pound) and a pound of sea bread. We marched a little distance and stopped "to refresh ourselves." We kindled some fires in the road, and some broiled their meat; as for myself, I ate mine raw. We quickly started on and marched till evening, when we went into a wood for the night. We did not pitch our tents, and about midnight it began to rain very hard, which soon put out all our fires and we had to lie "and weather it out." The troops marched again before day.

We continued our march until sometime after dark, when we arrived in the vicinity of the main army. We again turned into a wood for the night. The leaves and ground were as wet as water could make them. It was then foggy and the water dropping from the trees like a shower. We endeavored to get fire by flashing powder on the leaves, but this and every other expedient that we could employ failing, we were forced by our old master, Necessity, to lay down and sleep if we could, with three others

69

of our constant companions, Fatigue, Hunger, and Cold.

Next morning we joined the grand army near Philadelphia, and the heavy baggage being sent back to the rear of the army, we were obliged to put up huts by laying up poles and covering them with leaves, a capital shelter from winter storms. Here we continued to fast; indeed we kept a continual Lent. Ours was a real fast and, depend upon it, we were sufficiently mortified.

About this time the whole British army left the city and encamped on Chestnut Hill in our immediate neighborhood. We hourly expected an attack from them; we had a commanding position and were very sensible of it. We were kept constantly on the alert, and wished nothing more than to have them engage us, for we were sure of giving them a drubbing, being in excellent fighting trim, as we were starved and as cross and ill-natured as curs. The British, however, thought better of the matter, and, after several day's maneuvering on the hill, very civilly walked off into Philadelphia again.

Starvation seemed to be entailed upon the army and every animal connected with it. The oxen, brought from New England for draught, all died, and the southern horses fared no better; even the wild animals that had any concern with us suffered. A poor little squirrel, who had the ill luck to get cut off from the woods and fixing himself on a tree standing alone and surrounded by several of the soldier's huts, sat upon the tree till he starved to death and fell off the tree. He, however, got rid of his misery soon. He did not live to starve by piecemeal six or seven years.

Soon after the British had quit their position on Chestnut Hill, we left this place, and after marching and countermarching back and forward some days, we crossed the Schuylkill in a cold, rainy and snowy night [December 12] upon a bridge of wagons set end to end and joined together by boards and planks. And after a few days more maneuvering we at last settled down at a place called "the Gulf" and here we encamped some time. And here we had liked to have encamped forever—for starvation here *rioted* in its glory. But lest the reader should be disgusted at hearing so much said about "starvation," I will give something that, perhaps, may in some measure alleviate his ill humor.

While we lay here, there was a Continental Thanksgiving ordered by Congress. And as the army had all the cause in the world to be particularly thankful, if not for being well off, at least that it was no worse, we were ordered to participate in it. We had nothing to eat for two or three days previous, except what the trees of the fields and forests afforded us. But we must now have what Congress said, a sumptuous Thanksgiving to close the year of high living we had now nearly seen brought to a close. Well, to add something extraordinary to our present stock of provisions, our country, ever mindful of its suffering army, opened her sympathizing heart so wide, upon this occasion, as to give us some-

thing to make the world stare. And what do you think it was, reader? Guess. You cannot guess. I will tell you; it gave each and every man *half* a *gill* of rice and a *tablespoonful* of vinegar!!

After we had made sure of this extraordinary superabundant donation, we were ordered out to attend a meeting and hear a sermon delivered upon the happy occasion. I heard a sermon, a "thanksgiving sermon," what sort of one I do not know now, nor did I at the time I heard it. I had something else to think upon. My belly put me in remembrance of the fine Thanksgiving dinner I was to partake of when I could get it. I remember the text, like an attentive lad at church. I can *still* remember that it was this, "And the soldiers said unto him, And what shall we do? And he said unto them, Do violence to no man, nor accuse anyone falsely." The preacher ought to have added the remainder of the sentence to have made it complete, "And be content with your wages." But that would not do, it would be too apropos. However, he heard it as soon as the service was over. It was shouted from a hundred tongues.

Well, we had got through the services of the day and had nothing to do but to return in good order to our tents and fare as we could. As we returned to our camp, we passed by our commissary's quarters. All his stores, consisting of a barrel about two-thirds full of hocks of fresh beef, stood directly in our way, but there was a sentinel guarding even that. However, one of my messmates purloined a piece of it, four or five pounds perhaps. I was exceeding glad to see him take it. I thought it might help to eke out our Thanksgiving supper, but alas! how soon my expectations were blasted! The sentinel saw him have it as soon as I did and obliged him to return it to the barrel again. So I had nothing else to do but to go home and make out my supper as usual, upon a leg of nothing and no turnips.

The army was now not only starved but naked. The greatest part were not only shirtless and barefoot, but destitute of all other clothing, especially blankets. I procured a small piece of raw cowhide and made myself a pair of moccasins, which kept my feet (while they lasted) from the frozen ground, although, as I well remember, the hard edges so galled my ankles, while on a march, that it was with much difficulty and pain that I could wear them afterwards. The only alternative I had was to endure this inconvenience or to go barefoot, as hundreds of my companions had to, till they might be tracked by their blood upon the rough frozen ground. But hunger, nakedness and sore shins were not the only difficulties we had at that time to encounter. We had hard duty to perform and little or no strength to perform it with.

The army continued at and near the Gulf for some days, after which we marched for the Valley Forge in order to take up winter quarters. We were now in a truly forlorn condition—no clothing, no provisions and as disheartened as need be. We arrived, however, at our destination a few days before Christmas [December 18]. Our prospect was indeed dreary. In our miserable condition, to go into the wild woods and build us habitations to *stay* (not to *live*) in, in such a weak, starved and naked condition, was appalling in the highest degree, especially to New Englanders, unaccustomed to such kind of hardships at home.

However, there was no remedy, no alternative but this or dispersion. But dispersion, I believe, was not thought of, at least, I did not think of it. We had engaged in the defense of our injured country and we were determined to persevere as long as such hardships were not altogether intolerable. I had experienced what I thought sufficient of the hardships of a military life the year before, although nothing in comparison to what I had suffered the present campaign. We were now absolutely in danger of perishing in the midst of a plentiful country. We then had but little and often nothing to eat for days together; but now we had nothing and saw no likelihood of any betterment of our condition. Had there fallen deep snows or even heavy and long rainstorms, the whole army must inevitably have perished. Or had the enemy, strong and well provided as he then was, thought fit to pursue us, our poor emaciated carcasses must have "strewed the plain." But a kind and holy Providence took more notice and better care of us than did the country in whose service we were wearing away our lives by piecemeal.

We arrived at the Valley Forge in the evening. It was dark. There was no water to be found and I was perishing with thirst. I searched for water till I was weary and came to my tent without finding any. Fatigue and thirst, joined with hunger, almost made me desperate. I felt at that instant as if I would have taken victuals or drink from the best friend I had on earth by force. I am not writing fiction, all are sober realities. Just after I arrived at my tent, two soldiers, whom I did not know, passed by. They had some water in their canteens which they told me they had found a good distance off, but could not direct me to the place as it was very dark. I tried to beg a draught of water from them but they were as rigid as Arabs. At length I persuaded them to sell me a drink for three pence, Pennsylvania currency, which was every cent of property I could then call my own.

I lay here two nights and one day and had not a morsel of anything to eat all the time, save half of a small pumpkin, which I cooked by placing it upon a rock, the skin side uppermost, and making a fire upon it. By the time it was heated through I devoured it with as keen an appetite as I should a pie made of it at some other time.

The second evening after our arrival here, I was warned to be ready for a two days' command. I never heard a summons to duty with so much disgust before or since as I did that. How I could endure two days more fatigue without nourishment of some sort I could not tell, for I heard nothing said about "provisions." However, in the morning at roll call, I was obliged to comply. I went to the parade where I found a considerable number, ordered upon the same business, whatever it was. We were ordered to go to the quartermaster general and receive from him our final orders. We repaired to his quarters, which was about three miles from camp. Here we understood that our destiny was to go into the country on a foraging expedition, which was nothing more nor less than to procure provisions from the inhabitants for the men in the army and forage for the poor perishing cattle belonging to it, at the point of the bayonet.

We stayed at the quartermaster general's quarters till sometime in the afternoon, during which time a beef creature was butchered for us. I well remember what fine stuff it was. It was quite transparent. I thought at that time what an excellent lantern it would make. I was, notwithstanding, very glad to get some of it, bad as it looked. We got, I think, two days allowance of it and some sort of bread. We were then divided into several parties and sent off upon our expedition.

Our party consisted of a lieutenant, a sergeant, a corporal and eighteen privates. We marched till night when we halted and took up our quarters at a large farmhouse. We marched off early in the morning before the people of the house were stirring.

This day we arrived at Milltown, a small village halfway between Philadelphia and Lancaster, which was to be our quarters for the winter.

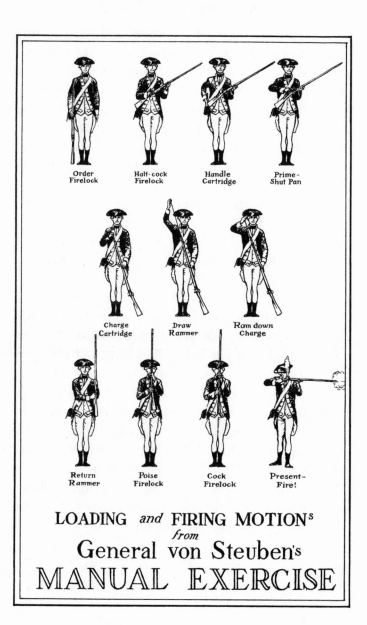

Order Firelock   Half-cock Firelock   Handle Cartridge   Prime-Shut Pan

Charge Cartridge   Draw Rammer   Ram down Charge

Return Rammer   Poise Firelock   Cock Firelock   Present-Fire!

LOADING *and* FIRING MOTIONᔆ
from
General von Steuben's
MANUAL EXERCISE

I V

The Campaign of 1778

Martin is trained by Baron von Steuben and goes on an expedition under General Lafayette to keep an eye on the British. He fights at Monmouth Court House on a hot June Sunday and sees Molly Pitcher at her cannon. He transfers to the Light Infantry, is nearly shot by his own sentries, and endures a hungry, cold winter.

As there was no cessation of duty in the army, I must commence another campaign as soon as the succeeding one is ended. There was no going home and spending the winter season among friends and procuring new strength and spirits. No, it was one constant drill, summer and winter. Like an old horse in a mill, it was a continual routine.

The first expedition I undertook in my new vocation was a foraging cruise. I was ordered off into the country in a party consisting of a corporal and six men.

We fared much better than I had ever done in the army before, or ever did afterwards. We had very good provisions all winter and generally enough of them. Some of us were constantly in the country with the wagons; we went out by turns and had no

79

one to control us. Our lieutenant scarcely ever saw
us or we him. Our sergeant never went out with us
once, all the time we were there, nor our corporal
but once. When we were in the country we were
pretty sure to fare well, for the inhabitants were remarkably kind to us. We had no guards to keep. Our
only duty was to help load the wagons with hay,
corn, meal, or whatever they were to take off, and to
keep them company till they arrived at the commissary's, at Milltown. From thence the articles were
carried to camp in other vehicles under other guards.

I do not remember that during the time I was employed in this business, which was from Christmas
to the latter part of April, ever to have met with the
least resistance from the inhabitants, take what we
would from their barns, mills, corncribs, or stalls.
But when we came to their stables, then look out for
the women! Take what horse you would, it was one
or the other's "pony," and they had no other to ride
to church. And when we had got possession of a
horse we were sure to have half a dozen or more
women pressing upon us, until by some means or
other they would slip the bridle from the horse's
head, and then we might catch him again if we
could. They would take no more notice of a charged
bayonet than a blind horse would of a cocked pistol.
It would answer no purpose to threaten to kill them
with the bayonet or musket. They knew as well as
we did that we would not put our threats in execution, and when they had thus liberated a horse, they
would laugh at us and ask why we did not do as we

threatened. Then they would generally ask us into their houses and treat us with as much kindness as though nothing had happened.

But the time at length came when we were obliged to go to camp for good and all, whether we chose it or not. An order from headquarters required all stationed parties and guards to be relieved, that all who had not had the smallpox might have an opportunity to have it before the warm weather came on. Accordingly about the last of April we were relieved by a party of southern troops. We marched off and arrived at camp the next day, much to the *seeming* satisfaction of our old messmates, and as much to the real dissatisfaction of ourselves. At least, it was so with me.

Thus far, since the year commenced, "Dame Fortune had been kind," but now "Miss-Fortune" was coming in for *her* set in the reel. I had now to enter again on my old system of starving; there was nothing to eat. I had brought two or three days' rations in my knapsack, and while that lasted I made shift to get along, but that was soon gone and I was then obliged to come to it again, which was sorely against my grain. During the past winter I had had enough to eat and been under no restraint. I had picked up a few articles of comfortable summer clothing among the inhabitants. Our lieutenant had never concerned himself about us; we had scarcely seen him during the whole time. When we were off duty we went when and where we pleased but now the scene was changed. We must go and come at bidding and suffer hunger besides.

82

The Campaign of 1778

After I had joined my regiment I was kept constantly, when off other duty, engaged in learning the Baron de Steuben's new Prussian exercise. It was a continual drill.

About this time I was sent off from camp in a detachment consisting of about three thousand men, with four fieldpieces, under the command of the young General Lafayette. We marched to Barren Hill, about twelve miles from Philadelphia. There are crossroads upon this hill, a branch of which leads to the city. We halted here, placed our guards, sent off our scouting parties, and waited for—I know not what. A company of about a hundred Indians, from some northern tribe, joined us here. There were three or four young Frenchmen with them. The Indians were stout-looking fellows and remarkably neat for that race of mortals, but they were Indians. There was upon the hill, and just where we were lying, an old church built of stone, entirely divested of all its entrails. The Indians were amusing themselves and the soldiers by shooting with their bows, in and about the church.

The next day I was one of a guard to protect the horses belonging to the detachment. They were in a meadow of six or eight acres, entirely surrounded by tall trees. It was cloudy and a low fog hung all night upon the meadow.

Just at the dawn of day the officers' waiters came, almost breathless, after the horses. Upon inquiring for the cause of the unusual hurry, we were told that the British were advancing upon us in our rear. How they could get there was to us a mystery, but they *were* there. We helped the waiters to catch their horses and immediately returned to the main body of the detachment. We found the troops all under arms and in motion, preparing for an onset. Those of the troops belonging to our brigade were put into the churchyard, which was enclosed by a wall of stone and lime about breast high, a good defense against musketry but poor against artillery. But our commander found that the enemy was too strong to be engaged in the position we then occupied. He therefore wisely ordered a retreat from this place to the Schuylkill, where we might choose any position that we pleased, having ragged woody hills in our rear and the river in front.

It was about three miles to the river. The weather was exceeding warm, and I was in the rear platoon of the detachment except two platoons of General Washington's Guards. The quick motion in front kept the rear on a constant trot. Two pieces of artillery were in front and two in the rear. The enemy had nearly surrounded us by the time our retreat commenced, but the road we were in was very favorable for us, it being for the most part and especially the first part of it through small woods and copses. When I was about halfway to the river, I saw the right wing of the enemy through a lawn about half a mile distant, but they were too late. Besides, they made a blunder here. They saw our rear guard with the two fieldpieces in its front, and thinking it the front of the detachment, they closed in to secure their prey, but when they had sprung their net they found that they had not a single bird under it.

We crossed the Schuylkill in good order, very near the spot where I had crossed it four times in the month of October the preceding autumn. As fast as the troops crossed they formed and prepared for action, and waited for them to attack us. But we saw no more of them that time, for before we had reached the river the alarm guns were fired in our camp and the whole army was immediately in motion.

The British, fearing that they should be outnumbered in their turn, directly set their faces for Philadelphia and set off in as much or more haste than we had left Barren Hill. They had, during the night, left the city with such silence and secrecy, and by taking what was called the New York road, that they escaped detection by all our parties. And the first knowledge [our parties] obtained of the enemy's movements was that he was upon their backs, between them and us on the hill.

The Indians, with all their alertness, had like to have "bought the rabbit." They kept coming in all the afternoon, in parties of four or five, whooping and hallooing like wild beasts. After they had got collected they vanished; I never saw any more of them. Our scouting parties all came in safe, but I was afterwards informed by a British deserter that several of the enemy perished by the heat and their exertions to get away from a retreating enemy.

The next day we crossed the Schuylkill again and went on to Barren Hill once more. We stayed there a day or two and then returned to camp with keen appetites and empty purses. If anyone asks why we did not stay on Barren Hill till the British came up, and have taken and given a few bloody noses—all I have to say is that General [Lafayette] well knew what he was about. He was not deficient in either courage or conduct, and that was well known to all the Revolutionary army.

Soon after this affair we left our winter cantonments, crossed the Schuylkill and encamped on the left bank of that river, just opposite to our winter quarters. We had lain here but a few days when we heard that the British army had left Philadelphia and were proceeding to New York, through the Jerseys. We marched immediately in pursuit. We crossed the Delaware at Coryell's Ferry, above Trenton, and encamped a day or two between that town and Princeton. Here I was again detached with a party of one thousand men, as light troops, to get into the enemy's route and follow him close, to favor desertion and pick up stragglers.

The day we were drafted [June 24] the sun was eclipsed. Had this happened upon such an occasion in "olden time," it would have been considered ominous either of good or bad fortune, but we took no notice of it.

Our detachment marched in the afternoon and towards night we passed through Princeton. Some of the patriotic inhabitants of the town had brought out to the end of the street we passed through some casks of ready-made toddy. It was dealt out to the men as they passed by, which caused the detachment to move slowly at this place. The young ladies of the town, and perhaps of the vicinity, had collected and were sitting in the stoops and at the windows to see the noble exhibition of a thousand half-starved and three-quarters naked soldiers pass in review before them. I chanced to be on the wing of a platoon next to the houses, as they were chiefly on one side of the street, and had a good chance to notice the ladies, and I declare that I never before nor since saw more beauty, considering the numbers, than I saw at that time. They were *all* beautiful.

We passed through Princeton and encamped on the open fields for the night, the canopy of heaven for our tent. Early next morning we marched again and came up with the rear of the British army. We followed them several days, arriving upon their camping ground within an hour after their departure from it. We had ample opportunity to see the devastation they made in their rout; cattle killed and lying about the fields and pastures, some just in the position they were in when shot down, others with a small spot of skin taken off their hind quarters and a mess of steak taken out; household furniture hacked and broken to pieces; wells filled up and mechanics' and farmers' tools destroyed. Such conduct did not give the Americans any more agreeable feelings toward them than they entertained before.

It was extremely hot weather, and the sandy plains of that part of New Jersey did not cool the air to any great degree, but we still kept close to the rear of the British army. Deserters were almost hourly coming over to us, but of stragglers we took only a few.

The next morning, as soon as the enemy began their march, we were again in motion and came to their last night's encamping ground just after sunrise. Here we halted an hour or two, as we often had to do, to give the enemy time to advance, our orders being not to attack them unless in self-defense. We were marching on as usual, when, about ten or eleven o'clock, we were ordered to halt and then to face to the rightabout. As this order was given by the officers in rather a different way than usual, we began to think something was out of joint somewhere, but what or where our united wisdom could not explain. The general opinion of the soldiers was that some part of the enemy had by some means got into our rear. We, however, retraced our steps till we came to our last night's encamping ground, when we left the route of the enemy and went off a few miles to a place called Englishtown.

It was uncommonly hot weather and we put up booths to protect us from the heat of the sun, which was almost insupportable. Whether we lay here one or two nights I do not remember. We were early in the morning mustered out and ordered to leave all our baggage under the care of a guard (our baggage was trifling), taking only our blankets and provisions (our provisions were less), and prepare for immediate march and action.

The officer who commanded the platoon that I belonged to was a captain, belonging to the Rhode

Island troops, and a fine brave man he was. He feared nobody nor nothing. When we were paraded, —"Now," said he to us, "you have been wishing for some days past to come up with the British. You have been wanting to fight. Now you shall have fighting enough before night."

The men did not need much haranguing to raise their courage, for when the officers came to order the sick and lame to stay behind as guards, they were forced to exercise their authority to the full extent before they could make even the invalids stay behind, and when some of their arms were about to be exchanged with those who were going into the field, they would not part with them. "If their arms went," they said, "*they* would go with them."

After all things were put in order, we marched, but halted a few minutes in the village [of Monmouth Court House], where we were joined by a few other troops, and then proceeded on. We now heard a few reports of cannon ahead. We went in a road running through a deep narrow valley, which was for a considerable way covered with thick wood. While in the wood we heard a volley or two of musketry, and upon inquiry we found it to be a party of our troops who had fired upon a party of British horse, but there was no fear of horse in the place in which we then were.

It was ten or eleven o'clock before we got through these woods and came into the open fields. The first cleared land we came to was an Indian cornfield, surrounded on the east, west and north sides by thick tall trees. The sun shining full upon the field, the soil of which was sandy, the mouth of a heated oven seemed to me to be but a trifle hotter than this plowed field; it was almost impossible to breathe. We had to fall back again as soon as we could, into the woods. By the time we had got under the shade of the trees and had taken breath, we received orders to retreat, as all the left wing of the army, that part being under the command of General [Charles] Lee, were retreating. Grating as this order was to our feelings, we were obliged to comply.

We had not retreated far before we came to a defile, a muddy, sloughy brook. While the artillery were passing this place, we sat down by the road-side. In a few minutes the Commander in Chief and suite crossed the road just where we were sitting. I heard him ask our officers "by whose order the troops were retreating," and being answered, "by General Lee's," he said something, but as he was moving forward all the time this was passing, he was too far off for me to hear it distinctly. Those that were nearer to him said that his words were "d——n him." Whether he did thus express himself or not I do not know. It was certainly very unlike him, but he seemed at the instant to be in a great passion.

His looks if not his words seemed to indicate as much. After passing us, he rode on to the plain field and took an observation of the advancing enemy. He remained there some time upon his old English charger, while the shot from the British artillery were rending up the earth all around him. After he had

taken a view of the enemy, he returned and ordered the two Connecticut brigades to make a stand at a fence, in order to keep the enemy in check while the artillery and other troops crossed the before-mentioned defile. When we had secured our retreat, the artillery formed a line of pieces upon a long piece of elevated ground. Our detachment formed directly in front of the artillery, as a covering party, so far below on the declivity of the hill that the pieces could play over our heads. And here we waited the approach of the enemy.

By this time the British had come in contact with the New England forces at the fence, when a sharp conflict ensued. These troops maintained their ground, till the whole force of the enemy had charged upon them through the fence. After being overpowered by numbers and the platoon officers had given orders for their several platoons to leave the fence, they had to force them to retreat, so eager were they to be revenged on the invaders of their country and rights.

As soon as the troops had left this ground the British planted their cannon upon the place and began a violent attack upon the artillery and our detachment, but neither could be routed. The cannonade continued for some time when the British pieces being mostly disabled, they reluctantly crawled back from the height which they had occupied and hid themselves from our sight.

Before the cannonade had commenced, a part of the right wing of the British army had advanced across a low meadow and brook and occupied an orchard on our left. The weather was almost too hot to live in, and the British troops in the orchard were forced by the heat to shelter themselves from it under the trees. We had a four-pounder on the left of our pieces which kept a constant fire upon the enemy during the whole contest.

After the British artillery had fallen back and the cannonade had mostly ceased in this quarter, and our detachment had an opportunity to look about us, Colonel [Joseph] Cilly of the New Hampshire Line, who was attached to our detachment, passed along in front of our line, inquiring for General Varnum's men, who were the Connecticut and Rhode Island men belonging to our command. We answered, "Here we are." He did not hear us in his hurry, but passed on. In a few minutes he returned, making the same inquiry. We again answered, "Here we are." "Ah!" said he, "you are the boys I want to assist in driving those rascals from yon orchard."

We were immediately ordered from our old detachment and joined another, the whole composing a corps of about five hundred men. We instantly marched towards the enemy's right wing, which was in the orchard, and kept concealed from them as long as possible by keeping behind the bushes. When we could no longer keep ourselves concealed, we marched into the open fields and formed our line. The British immediately formed and began to retreat to the main body of their army. Colonel Cilly, finding that we were not likely to overtake the enemy before they reached the main body of the army, on account of fences and other obstructions, ordered three or four platoons from the right of our corps to pursue and attack them, and thus keep them in play till the rest of the detachment could come up. I was in this party. We pursued without order. As I passed through the orchard I saw a number of the enemy lying under the trees, killed by our fieldpiece.

We overtook the enemy just as they were entering upon the meadow, which was rather bushy. When within about five rods of the rear of the retreating foe, I could distinguish everything about them. They were retreating in line, though in some disorder. I singled out a man and took my aim directly between his shoulders. (They were divested of their packs.) He was a good mark, being a broad-shouldered fellow. What became of him I know not; the fire and smoke hid him from my sight. One thing I know, that is, I took as deliberate aim at him as ever I did at any game in my life. But after all, I hope I did not kill him, although I intended to at the time.

By this time our whole party had arrived, and the British had obtained a position that suited them, as I suppose, for they returned our fire in good earnest, and we played the second part of the same tune. They occupied a much higher piece of ground than we did, and had a small piece of artillery, which the soldiers called a grasshopper. We had no artillery with us. The first shot they gave us from this piece cut off the thigh bone of a captain, just above the knee, and the whole heel of a private in the rear of

him. We gave it to poor Sawney (for they were
Scotch troops) so hot that he was forced to fall back
and leave the ground they occupied. When our commander saw them retreating and nearly joined with
their main body, he shouted, "Come, my boys, reload your pieces, and we will give them a set-off."
We did so, and gave them the parting salute, and the
firing on both sides ceased. We then laid ourselves
down under the fences and bushes to take breath,
for we had need of it. I presume everyone has heard
of the heat of that day, but none can realize it that
did not feel it. Fighting is hot work in cool weather,
how much more so in such weather as it was on the
twenty-eighth of June, 1778.

As soon as our party had ceased firing, it began in
the center, and then upon the right. As I was not in
that part of the army, I had no "adventure" in it,
but the firing was continued in one part or the other
of the field the whole afternoon. Our troops remained on the field all night with the Commander
in Chief. A regiment of Connecticut forces were sent
to lie as near the enemy as possible and to watch
their motions. If my readers wish to know how they
escaped so slyly without our knowledge, after such
precautions being used to prevent it, I must tell them
I know nothing about it.

One little incident happened during the heat of
the cannonade, which I was eyewitness to, and
which I think would be unpardonable not to mention. A woman whose husband belonged to the artillery and who was then attached to a piece in the

engagement, attended with her husband at the piece the whole time. While in the act of reaching a cartridge and having one of her feet as far before the other as she could step, a cannon shot from the enemy passed directly between her legs without doing any other damage than carrying away all the lower part of her petticoat. Looking at it with apparent unconcern, she continued her occupation.

The next day after the action we joined our regiments in the line and marched for Hudson's River. We marched by what was called "easy marches," that is, we struck our tents at three o'clock in the morning, marched ten miles and then encamped, which would be about one or two o'clock in the afternoon. Every third day we rested all day. In this way we went to King's Ferry, where we crossed the Hudson.

From King's Ferry the army proceeded to Tarrytown, and from thence to the White Plains. Here we drew some small supplies of summer clothing of which we stood in great need.

We lay at the White Plains some time. While here I was transferred to the Light Infantry, when I was immediately marched down to the lines. I had hard duty to perform during the remainder of the campaign.

There were three regiments of Light Infantry, composed of men from the whole main army. It was a motley group—Yankees, Irishmen, Buckskins and what not. The regiment that I belonged to was made up of about one half New Englanders and the remainder were chiefly Pennsylvanians—two sets of people as opposite in manners and customs as light and darkness. Consequently, there was not much cordiality subsisting between us, for, to tell the sober truth, I had in those days as lief have been incorporated with a tribe of western Indians as with any of the southern troops, especially of those which consisted mostly, as the Pennsylvanians did, of foreigners. But I *was* among them and in the same regiment too, and under their officers (but the officers, in general, were gentlemen) and had to do duty with them. To make a bad matter worse, I was often, when on duty, the only Yankee that happened to be on the same tour for several days together.

Our regiment was commanded by a Colonel [Richard] Butler, a Pennsylvanian. He was a brave officer, but a fiery, austere hothead. Whenever he had a dispute with a brother officer, and that was pretty often, he would never resort to pistols and swords, but always to his fists. I have more than once or twice seen him with a "black eye," and have seen other officers that he had honored with the same badge.

The duty of the Light Infantry is the hardest, while in the field, of any troops in the army, if there is any *hardest* about it. During the time the army keeps the field they are always on the lines near the enemy, and consequently always on the alert, constantly on the watch. Marching and guard-keeping, with all the other duties of troops in the field, fall plentifully to their share.

97

We lay at Bedford till the close of the season. Late in the autumn, the main army lay at New Milford, in the northwestern part of Connecticut. While there, the Connecticut troops drew some winter clothing. The men belonging to that state, who were in the Light Infantry, had none sent them. They, therefore, thought themselves hardly dealt by. Many of them, fearing they should lose their share of the clothing (of which they stood in great need), absconded from the camp at Bedford and went to New Milford. This caused our officers to keep patrolling parties around the camp during the night to prevent their going off. In consequence of this, I one evening nearly obtained a final discharge from the army.

I had been, in the afternoon, at a small brook in the rear of the camp, where the troops mostly got their water, to wash some clothes. Among the rest was a handkerchief, which I laid upon a stone or stump, and when I went to my tent I forgot to take it with me. Missing it after roll call, I went to the place to get it. It was almost dark, and quite so in the bushes. I was puzzled for some time to find the place, and longer before I could find the handkerchief. After finding it I did not hurry back, but loitered till the patrols were out, for I did not once think of them. It had now become quite dark, and I had to pass through a place where the soldiers had cut firewood. It was a young growth of wood, and the ground was covered with brush and the stumps about knee-high, quite thick. Just as I entered upon this spot I heard somebody challenge with "Who comes there?" I had no idea of being the person hailed, and kept very orderly on my way, blundering through the brush. I, however, received a second and third invitation to declare myself, but paid no attention to the request.

The next compliment I received was a shot from them. The ball passed very near to me but I still kept advancing, when instantly I had another salute. I then thought, that since I had been the cause of so much noise and alarm, it would be best for me to get off if possible, for I knew that if I was brought before our hotspur of a colonel I should "buy the rabbit." Accordingly, I put my best foot foremost. The patrol, which consisted of twelve or fifteen men, all had a hack at me, some of the balls passing very near me indeed. One in particular passed so near my head as to cause my ear to ring for some time after. I now sprang to it for dear life. But I had not made many leaps before I ran my knee with all my force against a white oak stump, which brought me up so short that I went heels over head over the stumps. I hardly knew whether I was dead or alive. However, I got up and blundered on till I reached my tent, into which I pitched and lay as still as the pain in my knee would allow me.

My messmates were all asleep and knew nothing of the affair then, nor did I ever let them or anyone else know of it till after the close of the campaign, when I had joined my regiment in the line and was clear of the southern officers. But my knee was in a fine pickle. The next morning it was swelled as big as my head, and lame enough. However, it did not long remain so. When I was questioned by the officers or any of the men how I came by my wound, I told them I fell down, and thus far I told the truth. But when anyone asked me how I came to fall down, I was compelled to equivocate a little.

The main army, about this time, quitted the eastern side of the Hudson River and passed into New Jersey, to winter quarters. The Connecticut and New Hampshire troops went to Redding and Danbury, in the western part of Connecticut. The Light Infantry, likewise, broke up their encampment at Bedford, and separated to join their respective regiments in the line.

We arrived at Redding about Christmas or a little before, and prepared to build huts for our winter quarters. And as I have got into winter quarters again, I will here bring my third campaign to a close.

V

The Campaign of 1779

Martin marches and countermarches, as the Continentals try to guess where the British will strike next. He enjoys a furlough, makes sport with some old wagon wheels and cannon shells, and suffers through the most frigid and prolonged winter of the century in a drafty log hut at Morristown.

We got settled in our winter quarters at the commencement of the new year and went on in our old Continental line of starving and freezing. We now and then got a little bad bread and salt beef (I believe chiefly horse-beef). The month of January was very stormy, a good deal of snow fell, and in such weather it was a mere chance if we got anything at all to eat. Our condition, at length, became insupportable. We concluded that we *could* not or *would* not bear it any longer. We were now in our own state [of Connecticut] and were determined that if our officers would not see some of our grievances redressed, the state should. Accordingly, one evening after roll calling, the men generally turned out, but without their arms, and paraded in front of their huts. We had no need of informing the officers. We well knew that they would hear of our muster without our troubling ourselves to inform them.

We had hardly got paraded, before all our officers, with the colonel at their head, came in front of the regiment, expressing a deal of sorrow for the hardships we were compelled to undergo, but much more for what they were pleased to call our mutinous conduct. This latter expression of their sorrow only served to exasperate the men, which the officers observing, changed their tone and endeavored to soothe the Yankee temper they had excited, and, with an abundance of fair promises, persuaded us to return to our quarters again.

But hunger was not to be so easily pacified, and would not suffer many of us to sleep. We were therefore determined that none others should sleep. Martial law was very strict against firing muskets in camp. Nothing could, therefore, raise the officers' "lofty ideas" sooner, or more, than to fire in camp; but it was beyond the power or vigilance of all the officers to prevent the men from "making void the law" on that night. Finding they were watched by the officers, they got an old gun barrel which they placed in a hut that was unfinished. This they loaded a third part full and putting a slow match to it, would then escape to their own huts, when the old barrel would speak for itself, with a voice that would be heard. The officers would then muster out, and some running and scolding would ensue; but none knew who made the noise, or where it came from.

This farce was carried on the greater part of the
night; but at length the officers, getting tired of running so often to catch Mr. Nobody without finding
him, gave up the chase, and the men, seeing they
could no longer gull the officers, gave up the business
likewise.

We fared a little better for a few days after this
memento to the officers, but it soon became an old
story and the old system commenced again. We
endeavored to bear it with our usual fortitude, until
it again became intolerable, and the soldiers deter-

mined to try once more to raise some provisions, if not, at least to raise another dust.

Accordingly, one evening, after dark, we all turned out with our arms, appointed a commander and were determined, if we could not be better accommodated, to march into the center of the state and disperse to our homes, in presence of as many of our fellow citizens as chose to be spectators. After we had organized ourselves and regulated the plan for our future operations, it was the design of our regiment to have marched to our field officers' quarters, and through them to demand of our country better usage. But before we had got all our little matters settled, our adjutant came up and, seeing us in arms upon the parade at that time of night, mistrusted something was in the wind. He passed us without saying a word and went directly and informed the other officers, all of whom were soon upon the parade.

Our major was the first that arrived. He was a fine, bold-looking man, and made a fine appearance. He came on to the right of the regiment, and soon after the colonel and other officers came in front. The commanding sergeant ordered the men to shoulder arms and then to present (which is a token of respect) and then to order them again. The major then addressed the sergeant thus: "Well, Sergeant ———— you have got a larger regiment than we had this evening at roll call, but I should think it would be more agreeable for the men to be asleep in their huts this cold night, than to be standing on the parade, for I remember that they were very impatient at roll call on account of the cold."

"Yes, sir," said the sergeant, "Solomon says that 'the abundance of the rich will not suffer *him* to sleep,' and we find that the abundance of poverty will not suffer us to sleep." By this time the colonel had come to where the major and sergeant were arguing the case, and the old mode of flattery and promising was resorted to and produced the usual effect. We all once more returned to our huts and fires, and there spent the remainder of the night, muttering over our forlorn condition.

It was now the beginning of February. Many of the men had obtained furloughs to go home and visit their friends, before I had left the Light Infantry, and many since. I now made application and obtained one for fifteen days' absence. I prepared for the journey, which was about thirty miles, and started from the camp about nine o'clock in the morning, intending to go the whole distance that day. I had not a mouthful of anything to eat or to carry with me. I had, it is true, two or three shillings of old Continental money, worth about as much as its weight in rags. I, however, set off for home.

I believe the old people were glad to see me. They appeared to be much so, and I am quite sure I was glad to see them and all my other friends. I had now an opportunity of seeing the place of my boyhood, visit old acquaintance, and ramble over my old haunts. But my time was short, and I had, of course, to employ every minute to the best advantage.

105

I remained at home till my furlough had fully expired. I intended my country should give me a day to return to camp. The day before I intended to set off for the army, my lieutenant arrived at home to spend a week with his family. He called upon me and told me that if I chose I might stay and accompany him to camp, and he would be responsible for me. I did not want much persuasion to comply with his desire, and accordingly remained another week and then went with the lieutenant to camp and had no fault found.

I had not been at camp more than a week before I was sent off with a large detachment to New London to guard the fortifications in and about that town. On our march we passed through the place of my residence. The detachment tarried a night there, so I had an opportunity of being at home another night.

We went by easy marches and nothing of consequence occurred until we arrived at New London. Here we were put into houses, and here, too, we almost starved to death, and I believe should have quite starved, had we not found some clams. We had nothing to eat except now and then a little miserable beef or a little fresh fish and a very little bread, baked by a baker belonging to the town, which had some villainous drug incorporated with it that took all the skin off our mouths. I sincerely believe it was done on purpose to prevent our eating. I was not free from a sore mouth the whole time I stayed there.

We stayed here, starving, until the first of May,

when we received orders to march to camp and join our regiments. The troops belonging to New Hampshire marched sometime before we did. While on our march, we halted in a village. Here I went into a house, with several other soldiers, which happened to be a deacon's. While there some of the men chanced to swear (a circumstance extremely uncommon with the soldiers), upon which the good woman of the house checked them. "Is there any harm in it?" said one of them. "Yes," said she. "Well," said he, "may I not say swamp it?" "No," said she, "nor maple log roll over me, neither."

We went on to New Haven where we arrived upon a Sabbath eve and stayed till Wednesday. On the Tuesday following there was to be a muster of the militia. On Monday we washed our clothes and, as we understood we were to remain here during the next day, we put ourselves into as decent a condition as we possibly could to witness the militia exhibition the next day. Early next morning, there was a general stir in the town, a regiment of foot and a troop of horse were paraded on the green, and they made a very good appearance (considering the times), to speak the truth; but they seemed to be rather shy of displaying their knowledge of military tactics before regular troops. However, they did very well and deserved praise, whether they received it or not.

The next morning we marched again. I obtained permission to go in advance of the troops and see my grandparents again. I would have done this sooner, but I could not forego the pleasure of seeing the

militia muster. I remained at home that day and the
next, and then started for camp. I was acquainted
with the country, and consequently could reach
camp by a much shorter way than the troops, by
which means I arrived there within a few hours after
them.

We remained here a short time after my return
from New London when we received information
that the British were moving up the Hudson River
in force, had taken possession of Stony Point, and
were fortifying it. We were immediately ordered to
march. We went directly to the Fishkill, on the Hudson, and from thence down nearly opposite to West
Point. We remained here some days. I was the most
of that time on a stationed guard, keeping the horses
that belonged to the army at pasture.

After being relieved from this guard, I was detached with a small party to the Peekskill, in the
southern edge of the Highlands. We took up our
quarters in some old barracks. There was a number
of bombshells and some old damaged wagon wheels
lying near the barracks. One day, [we diverted] ourselves by filling the shells with water, plugging them
up, and setting them on the fire. The water boiling,
the steam would force the plug out with a report as
loud as that of a pistol.

Tired with exercising ourselves at this diversion,
we began to contrive some other mischief. Four or
five of us took one of the old wagon wheels and,
after considerable trouble and fatigue, carried the
wheel about thirty or forty rods up the mountain,

at the back of the barracks and a considerable distance from them, when we gave the wheel the liberty to shift for itself and find its own way back. It went very regular for a few turns, when taking a glancing stroke against something, it took a course directly for the barracks and just in that part, too, where the men were, who we could hear distinctly laughing and talking. Ah me! What would I not have given had I never meddled with the ugly thing, but it was then too late to repent. I confess I felt myself in a forlorn case. The barracks were only a single board thick, and those rotten and old, and the wheel might have gone through them and the men, too, without scarcely retarding its progress. We all stood breathless, waiting the result, when, as it happened, the wheel, when within about fifteen feet of the barracks, and with the motion almost of a cannon ball, struck something that gave it an elevation of twenty or thirty feet into the air, and passed over the barracks and several rods beyond before it struck the ground again. The reader may rest satisfied that this last circumstance did not cause many tears of grief to fall.

The Americans had a fortification upon Verplanck's Point, on the eastern side of the Hudson, opposite Stony Point, garrisoned by a captain and about one hundred men. The British took this place and made the garrison prisoners, after a close siege of about a week, and fortified the Point. They appeared, by their conduct, to have a strong inclination to possess West Point. To make a diversion in their own favor and draw off some of our forces from the vicinity of that fortress, they sent the infamous Governor [William] Tryon into Connecticut with his banditti, who took possession first of New Haven and plundered it, and then embarked and went and plundered and burnt Fairfield and Norwalk. The two Connecticut brigades were then sent in pursuit of them. We marched nearly down to the seacoast when, the enemy getting scent of us, they took to

their shipping and made the best of their way back
to New York. We returned as soon as possible.

Being on our march the fifteenth day of July and
destitute of all kinds of eatables, just at night I ob-
served a cheese in a press before a farmer's door.
We, being about to halt for the night, I determined
to return after dark and lay siege to it. But we went
further than I expected before we halted, and a
smart shower of rain with thunder happening at the
time, the cheese escaped. It cleared off with a brisk
wind at northwest and cold. We were all wet to the
skin and had no tents with us, lying on the western
side of a cleared hill. I never came nearer perishing
with the cold in the middle of summer in all my life.

In the night we heard the cannon at Stony Point,
and early next morning had information of the taking of that place by the Light Infantry of our army
under the command of General [Anthony] Wayne.
Our officers were all on tiptoe to show their abilities
in executing some extraordinary exploit. Verplanck's
Point was the word. "Shall the Light Infantry get all
the honor, and we do nothing!" said they. Accordingly, we set off, full tilt, to take Verplanck's Point.
We marched directly for the Peekskill and arrived
near there early in the day. We there received information that the British at Verplanck's Point were reinforced and advancing to attack *us*. We were quite
knocked on the head by this news. However, we put
ourselves in as good a condition as our circumstances
would admit and waited their approach. They were

afraid of us, or we of them, or both, for we did not come in contact that time. And thus ended the taking of Verplanck's Point and our honorable expectations.

We then fell back and encamped, but soon after we broke up our encampment and fell back to Robinson's farm just below West Point, on the eastern side of the river. Here we lay the rest of the season, employed in building two strong bombproof redoubts on two hills near the river. Sometime late in the fall, the British evacuated all their works and retired to New York. A large detachment, of which I was one, was sent to Verplanck's Point to level the British works. We were occupied in this business nearly two weeks, working and starving by day, and at night having to lie in the woods without tents.

We remained at and near Peekskill till sometime in the month of December. The cold weather having commenced earlier than usual, we had hard combating with hunger, cold, nakedness and hard duty, but were obliged to grapple with them all as well as we could. As the old woman said to her husband, when she baked him instead of his clothes, to kill the vermin, "You must grin and bear it."

About the middle of this month we crossed the Hudson at King's Ferry and proceeded into New Jersey for winter quarters. Our destination was a place called Basking Ridge [near Morristown].

It was cold and snowy. We had to march all day through the snow and at night take up our lodgings in some wood, where, after shoveling away the snow, we used to pitch three or four tents facing each other, and then join in making a fire in the center. Sometimes we could procure an armful of buckwheat straw to lie upon, which was deemed a luxury. Provisions, as usual, took up but a small part of our time, though much of our thoughts.

We arrived on our wintering ground in the latter part of the month of December, and once more, like the wild animals, began to make preparations to build us a "city for habitation." The soldiers, when immediately going about the building of their winter huts, would always endeavor to provide themselves with such tools as were necessary for the business (it is no concern of the reader's, as I conceive, by what means they procured their tools), such as crosscut saws, handsaws, frows, augers, &c. to expedite the erection and completion of their dwelling places. Do not blame them too much, gentle reader, if you should chance to make a shrewd Yankee guess how they *did* procure them; remember, they were in distress, and you know when a man is in that condition he will not be over scrupulous how he obtains relief.

We encamped near our destined place of operation and immediately commenced. It was upon the southerly declivity of a hill. The snow was more than a foot deep, and the weather none of the warmest. We had to level the ground to set our huts upon; the soil was a light loam. When digging just below the frost, which was not deep, the snow having fallen early in the season, we dug out a number of toads, that would

113

hop off when brought to the light of day as lively as in summertime. We found by this where toads take up their winter quarters, if we can never find where swallows take up theirs.

As this will be the last time that I shall have occasion to mention my having to build huts for our winter habitations, I will, by the reader's leave, just give a short description of the fashion and manner of erecting one of those log towns.

After the ground was marked out by the quartermasters, much after the same manner as for pitching tents in the field, we built the huts in the following manner: Four huts, two in front and two in the rear, then a space of six or eight feet, when four more huts were placed in the same order, and so on to the end of the regiment, with a parade in front and a street through the whole, between the front and rear, the whole length, twelve or fifteen feet wide. Next in order, in the rear of these huts, the officers of the companies built theirs with their waiters in the rear of them. Next the field officers in the same order. Every two huts, that is, one in front and one in the rear, had just their width in front indefinitely, and no more, to procure the materials for building; the officers had all in the rear. No one was allowed to transgress these bounds on any account whatever, either for building or firewood.

The next thing is the erecting of the huts. They were generally about twelve by fifteen or sixteen feet square, all uniformly of the same dimensions. The building of them was thus: after procuring the most

suitable timber for the business, it was laid up by notching them in at the four corners. When arrived at the proper height, about seven feet, the two end sticks which held those that served for plates were made to jut out about a foot from the sides, and a straight pole made to rest on them, parallel to the plates; the gable ends were then formed by laying on pieces with straight poles on each, which served for ribs to hold the covering, drawing in gradually to the ridgepole. Now for the covering: this was done by sawing some of the larger trees into cuts about four feet in length, splitting them into bolts, and riving them into shingles, or rather staves; the covering then commenced by laying on those staves, resting the lower ends on the poles by the plates; they were laid on in two thicknesses, carefully breaking joints. These were then bound on by a straight pole with withes, then another double tier with the butts resting on this pole and bound on as before, and so on to the end of the chapter. A chimney was then built at the center of the back side, composed of stone as high as the eaves and finished with sticks and clay, if clay was to be had, if not, with mud. The last thing was to hew stuff and build us up cabins or berths to sleep in, and then the buildings were fitted for the reception of *gentleman soldiers*, with all their *rich* and *gay* furniture.

Such were the habitations we had to construct at this time. We got into them about the beginning of the year, when the weather became intensely cold. Cold weather and snow were plenty, but beef and bread were extremely scarce in the army. Let it be recollected that this was what has been termed the "hard winter," and hard it was to the poor soldiers. So here I will close the narrative of my campaign of 1779. And happy should I then have thought myself if that had ended the war, but I had to see a little more trouble before that period arrived.

VI

The Campaign of 1780

Martin's regiment joins a detachment that crosses frozen New York Bay in sleighs to attack the British on Staten Island. He nearly starves at Morristown before spring comes, joins his companions in an ugly mutiny, and becomes a sergeant in the Corps of Sappers and Miners.

The winter of 1779 and '80 was very severe. It has been denominated "the hard winter." And hard it was to the army in particular, in more respects than one. The period of the Revolution has repeatedly been styled "the times that tried men's souls." I often found that those times not only tried men's souls, but their bodies too; I know they did mine.

Sometime in January there happened a spell of remarkably cold weather. In the height of the cold, a large detachment from the army was sent on an expedition against some fortifications held by the British on Staten Island. It was supposed by our officers that the bay before New York was frozen sufficiently to prevent any succors being sent to the garrisons. It was therefore determined to endeavor to surprise them and get possession of their fortifica-

118

tions before they could obtain help. Accordingly, our troops were all conveyed in sleighs and other carriages, but the enemy got intelligence of our approach (doubtless by some Tory) before our arrival on the island. When we arrived we found Johnny Bull prepared for our reception. We could not surprise them, and to take their works by storm looked too hazardous. To besiege them in regular form was out of the question, as the bay was not frozen so much as we expected. There was an armed brig lying in the ice not far from the shore. She received a few shots from our fieldpieces for a morning's salutation. We then fell back a little distance and took up our abode for the night upon a bare bleak hill, in full rake of the northwest wind, with no other covering or shelter than the canopy of the heavens, and no fuel but some old rotten rails which we dug up through the snow, which was two or three feet deep. The weather was cold enough to cut a man in two.

We lay on this accommodating spot till morning when we began our retreat from the island. The British were quickly in pursuit. They attacked our rear guard and made several of them prisoners. We arrived at camp after a tedious and cold march of many hours, some with frozen toes, some with frozen fingers and ears, and half-starved into the bargain. Thus ended our Staten Island expedition.

Soon after this there came several severe snowstorms. At one time it snowed the greater part of four days successively, and there fell nearly as many feet deep of snow. We were absolutely, literally

starved. I do solemnly declare that I did not put a single morsel of victuals into my mouth for four days and as many nights, except a little black birch bark which I gnawed off a stick of wood, if that can be called victuals. I saw several of the men roast their old shoes and eat them, and I was afterwards informed by one of the officers' waiters, that some of the officers killed and ate a favorite little dog that belonged to one of them. If this was not "suffering" I request to be informed what can pass under that name. If "suffering" like this did not "try men's souls," I confess that I do not know what could. The fourth day, just at dark, we obtained a half pound of lean fresh beef and a gill of wheat for each man. Whether we had any salt to season so delicious a morsel I have forgotten, but I am sure we had no bread, except the wheat. But I will assure the reader that we had the best of sauce; that is, we had keen appetites. When the wheat was so swelled by boiling as to be beyond the danger of swelling in the stomach, it was deposited there without ceremony.

After this, we sometimes got a little beef, but no bread. We, however, once in a while got a little rice, but as to flour or bread, I do not recollect that I saw a morsel of either (I mean wheaten) during the winter, all the bread kind we had was Indian meal.

We continued here, starving and freezing, until, I think, sometime in February, when the two Connecticut brigades were ordered to the lines near Staten Island. The small parties from the army which had been sent to the lines were often surprised and taken by the enemy or cut to pieces by them. These circumstances, it seems, determined the Commander in Chief to have a sufficient number of troops there to withstand the enemy even should they come in considerable force.

The First Brigade took up its quarters in a village called Westfield, and the Second in another called Springfield. We were put into the houses with the inhabitants.

I think it necessary to give some information of the nature and kind of duty we had to perform while here, that the reader may form a clearer idea of the hardships we had to encounter in the discharge of it. I shall speak only of the First Brigade, as I belonged to that.

We were stationed about six miles from Elizabeth-town, which is situated near the waters which sep-arate Staten Island from the main. We had to send a detachment to this place which continued on duty there several days. It consisted of about two hun-dred men, and had to form several guards while there. We had another guard, which consisted of about one hundred men, at a place called Wood-bridge. This guard stayed there two days before they were relieved, and was ten miles from our quarters. Woodbridge also lay by the same waters. We like-wise kept a quarter guard in every regiment at home, besides other small guards.

Our duty all the winter and spring was thus. Sup-pose I went upon the Woodbridge guard. I must march from the parade at eight o'clock in the morn-ing, go a distance of ten miles and relieve the guard already there, which would commonly bring it to about twelve o'clock; stay there two days and two nights, then be relieved and take up the afternoon of that day to reach our quarters at Westfield, where, as soon as I could get into my quarters, and, gener-ally, before I could lay by my arms, warned for Elizabethtown the next day. Thus it was the whole time we lay here, which was from the middle of Feb-ruary to the latter part of May following. It was Woodbridge and Elizabethtown, Elizabethtown and Woodbridge, alternately, till I was absolutely sick of hearing the names mentioned.

The guard kept at Woodbridge, being so small and so far from the troops and so near the enemy, was obliged to be constantly on the alert. We had three different houses that we occupied alternately during the night: the first was an empty house, the second the parson's house, and the third a farmer's house. We had to remove from one to the other three times every night, from fear of being surprised by the enemy.

There was no trusting the inhabitants, for many of them were friendly to the British, and we did not know who were or who were not, and consequently, were distrustful of them all, unless it were one or two. The parson was a staunch Whig, as the friends to the country were called in those times, and the farmer was another, and perhaps more that we were not acquainted with. Be that as it would, we were shy of trusting them. Here, especially in the night, we were obliged to keep about one half of the guard upon sentry, and besides these, small patrolling parties on all the roads leading towards the enemy. But with all the vigilance we could exercise, we could hardly escape being surprised and cut off by the enemy. They exerted themselves more than common to take some of our guards, because we had challenged them to do it, and had bid them defiance.

I was once upon this guard. It was in the spring, after the snow had gone off the ground. Myself and another young man took for our tour of duty to patrol upon a certain road during the night. About midnight or a little after, our guard being then at the farmer's house, which was the farthest back from the water's side of any of the houses we occupied, caused some of our sentinels to be three miles from the guard. We patrolled from the guard to the farthest sentries which were two (or in military phrase, a double sentinel) who were standing upon a bridge. After we had visited these sentinels and were returning, we passed the parson's house. There was a muddy plash in the road nearly opposite the house, and as it happened, the man with me passed on the side next to the house and I passed on the other. After we had got clear of the water and had come together again, he told me there were British soldiers lying in the garden and dooryard. I asked him if he was sure. He said, "I was near enough to have reached them with my hand, had there been no fence between."

We stopped and consulted what was best for us to do. I was for going back and giving them a starter, but my comrade declined. He thought it would be best to return to the guard and inform the officers what we had discovered, and let them act their pleasure. We accordingly did so, when the captain of the guard sent down two horsemen to ascertain whether it was as we had reported. The horsemen, finding it true, instead of returning and informing the officers, as they were ordered to, fired their carbines, one into the house, the ball lodging in the bedpost where the parson and his wife were in bed, and the other into the garden or dooryard. The British, finding they were discovered, walked off without even returning a single shot. We were sorry then that we had not given them a loving salute as we passed them, and thus saved the horsemen the trouble. This was one among many of the sly methods the British took to surprise and take our guards.

We remained on this tedious duty, getting nothing to eat but our old fare, Indian meal, and not over much of that, till the middle of May, when we were relieved, but we remained at our quarters eight or ten days after that. Our duty was not quite so hard now as it had been, but that faithful companion, Hunger, stuck as close to us as ever.

We left Westfield about the twenty-fifth of May and went to Basking Ridge to our old winter cantonments. We did not reoccupy the huts we built, but some others that the troops had left. Here, the monster Hunger, still attended us. He was not to be shaken off by any efforts we could use, for here was the old story of starving, as rife as ever. We had entertained some hopes that when we had left the lines and joined the main army, we should fare a little better, but we found that there was no betterment in the case. For several days after we rejoined the army, we got a little musty bread and a little beef, about every other day, but this lasted only a short time and then we got nothing at all. The men were now exasperated beyond endurance. They could not stand it any longer. They saw no alternative but to starve to death, or break up the army, give all up and go home. This was a hard matter for the soldiers to think upon. They were truly patriotic, they loved their country, and they had already suffered everything short of death in its cause. And now, after such extreme hardships to give up all was too much, but to starve to death was too much also. What was to be done? Here was the army starved and naked, and there their country sitting still and expecting the army to do notable things while fainting from sheer starvation. All things considered, the army was not to be blamed. Reader, suffer what we did and you will say so, too.

We had borne as long as human nature could endure, and to bear longer we considered folly. Accordingly, one pleasant day, the men spent the most of their time upon the parade, growling like soreheaded dogs. At evening roll call they began to show their dissatisfaction by snapping at the officers and acting contrary to their orders. After their dismissal from the parade, the officers went, as usual, to their quarters, except the adjutant, who happened to remain, giving details for next day's duty to the orderly sergeants. The men, none of whom had left the parade, began to make him sensible that they had something in train. He said something that did not altogether accord with the soldiers' ideas of propriety. One of the men retorted. The adjutant called him a mutinous rascal, or some such epithet, and then left the parade. This man, then stamping the butt of his musket upon the ground, as much as to say, I am in a passion, called out, "Who will parade with me?" The whole regiment immediately fell in and formed.

We had made no plans for our future operations,

but while we were consulting how to proceed, the Fourth Regiment, which lay on our left, formed, and came and paraded with us. We now concluded to go in a body to the other two regiments [the Third and Sixth] that belonged to our brigade and induce them to join with us. These regiments lay forty or fifty rods in front of us, with a brook and bushes between. We did not wish to have anyone in particular to command, lest he might be singled out for a court-martial. We therefore gave directions to the drummers to give certain signals on the drums. At the first signal we shouldered our arms, at the second we faced, at the third we began our march to join with the other two regiments, and went off with music playing.

By this time our officers had obtained knowledge of our military maneuvering and some of them had run across the brook, by a nearer way than we had taken, it being now quite dark, and informed the officers of those regiments of our approach and supposed intentions. The officers ordered their men to parade as quick as possible *without* arms. When that was done, they stationed a camp guard, that happened to be near at hand, between the men and their huts, which prevented them from entering and taking their arms, which they were very anxious to do. Colonel [Return Jonathan] Meigs, of the Sixth Regiment, exerted himself to prevent his men from obtaining their arms until he received a severe wound in his side by a bayonet in the scuffle, which cooled his courage at the time. He said he had al-

127

ways considered himself the soldier's friend and thought the soldiers regarded him as such, but had reason now to conclude he might be mistaken. Colonel Meigs was truly an excellent man and a brave officer. The man, whoever he was, that wounded him, doubtless had no particular grudge against him. It was dark and the wound was given, it is probable, altogether unintentionally.

When we found the officers had been too crafty for us, we returned with grumbling instead of music, the officers following in the rear growling in concert. One of the men in the rear calling out, "Halt in front," the officers seized upon him like wolves on a sheep and dragged him out of the ranks, intending to make an example of him for being a "mutinous rascal." But the bayonets of the men pointing at their breasts as thick as hatchel teeth compelled them quickly to relinquish their hold of him. We marched back to our own parade and then formed again. The officers now began to coax us to disperse to our quarters, but that had no more effect upon us than their threats. One of them slipped away into the bushes, and after a short time returned, counterfeiting to have come directly from headquarters. Said he, "There is good news for you, boys, there has just arrived a large drove of cattle for the army."

But this piece of finesse would not avail. All the answer he received for his labor was, "Go and butcher them," or some such slight expression. The lieutenant colonel of the Fourth Regiment now came on to the parade. He could persuade *his* men, he said, to go peaceably to their quarters. After a good deal of palaver, he ordered them to shoulder their arms, but the men taking no notice of him or his order, he fell into a violent passion, threatening them with the bitterest punishment if they did not immediately obey his orders. He again ordered them to shoulder their arms, but he met with the same success that he did at the first trial. He therefore gave up the contest and walked off to his quarters, chewing the cud of resentment all the way, and how much longer I neither knew nor cared. The rest of the officers, after they found that they were likely to meet with no better success than the colonel, walked off likewise to their huts.

While we were under arms, the Pennsylvania troops, who lay not far from us, were ordered under arms and marched off their parades upon, as they were told, a secret expedition. They had surrounded us, unknown to either us or themselves (except the officers). At length, getting an item of what was going forward, they inquired of some of the stragglers what was going on among the Yankees. Being informed that they had mutinied on account of the scarcity of provisions, "Let us join them," said they. "Let us join the Yankees; they are good fellows, and have no notion of lying here like fools and starving." Their officers needed no further hinting. The troops were quickly ordered back to their quarters, from fear that they would join in the same song with the Yankees. We knew nothing of all this for some time afterwards.

After our officers had left us to our own option, we dispersed to our huts and laid by our arms of our own accord, but the worm of hunger gnawing so keen kept us from being entirely quiet. We, therefore, still kept upon the parade in groups, venting our spleen at our country and government, then at our officers, and then at ourselves for our imbecility in staying there and starving for an ungrateful people who did not care what became of us, so they could enjoy themselves while we were keeping a cruel enemy from them. While we were thus venting our gall against we knew not who, Colonel [Walter] Stewart of the Pennsylvania Line, with two or three other officers of that Line, came to us and questioned us respecting our unsoldierlike conduct (as he termed it). We told him he needed not to be informed of the cause of our present conduct, but that we had borne till we considered further forbearance pusillanimity; that the times, instead of mending, were growing worse; and finally, that we were determined not to bear or forbear much longer. We were unwilling to desert the cause of our country, when in distress; that we knew her cause involved our own, but what signified our perishing in the act of saving her, when that very act would inevitably destroy us, and she must finally perish with us.

"Why do you not go to your officers," said he, "and complain in a regular manner?" We told him we had repeatedly complained to them, but they would not hear us. "Your officers," said he, "are gentlemen, they *will* attend to you. I know them; they cannot refuse to hear you. But your officers suffer as much as you do. We all suffer. The officers have no money to purchase supplies with any more than the private men have, and if there is nothing in the public store we must fare as hard as you. I have no other resources than you have to depend upon. I had not a sixpence to purchase a partridge that was offered me the other day. Besides," said he, "you know not how much you injure your own characters by such conduct. You Connecticut troops have won immortal honor to yourselves the winter past, by your perseverance, patience, and bravery, and now you are shaking it off at your heels. But I will go and see your officers, and talk with them myself." He went, but what the result was, I never knew. This Colonel Stewart was an excellent officer, much beloved and respected by the troops of the line he belonged to. He possessed great personal beauty; the Philadelphia ladies styled him *the Irish Beauty*.

Our stir did us some good in the end, for we had provisions directly after, so we had no great cause for complaint for some time.

About this time there were about three thousand men ordered out for a particular field day, for the Prussian General Baron de Steuben to exercise his maneuvering functions upon. We marched off our regimental parades at dawn of day, and went three or four miles to Morristown to a fine plain, where we performed a variety of military evolutions. We were furnished with a plenty of blank cartridges, had eight or ten fieldpieces, and made a great noise, if nothing more.

In the month of June, five thousand British and Hessian troops advanced into New Jersey, burnt several houses in Elizabethtown and the Presbyterian meetinghouse and most of the village of Springfield. They also barbarously murdered, by shooting the wife of the minister of that place. What their further intentions were could not be ascertained by our commanders. Sometimes it was conjectured that they were aiming at a quantity of public stores deposited in Morristown; sometimes that it was for a diversion in favor of their main army, by endeavoring to amuse us till their forces could push up the North River and attack West Point. Our army was accordingly kept in a situation to relieve either in case of an attack. While we remained in this situation our army was infested by spies from the British. I saw three of those vermin, one day, hanging on one gallows. The enemy soon after recoiled into their shell again at New York.

After the British had retreated to New York, our army marched for West Point.

The Connecticut forces crossed the river to the eastern side and encamped opposite to West Point, upon what was called Nelson's Point. It was now very hot weather, being the latter part of June. Here, for a considerable length of time, our rations, when we got any, consisted of bread and salt shad. This fish, as salt as fire, and dry bread, without any kind of vegetables, was hard fare in such extreme hot weather as it was then. We were compelled to eat it as it was. If we attempted to soak it in a brook that ran close by the camp, we were quite sure to lose it, there being a great abundance of otters and minks in and about the water, four-legged and two-legged (but much the largest number of the latter), so that they would be quite sure to carry off the fish, let us do what we would to prevent it.

And now there was to be a material change in my circumstances, which, in the long run, was much in my favor. There was a small corps to be raised by enlistments; and in case of the failure of that, by drafts from the line. These men were called "Sappers and Miners," to be attached to the engineer's department. I had known of this for some time, but never had a thought of belonging to it, although I had heard our major tell some of our officers that if there was a draft from our regiment, he intended I should go, although, he added, he did not wish to part with me. I, however, thought no more about it, till a captain of that corps applied for a draft of one man from each regiment throughout the whole army present. The captain was personally acquainted with our major and told him he would like to have him furnish a man from the regiment that he knew was qualified for a non-commissioned officer. The major then pitched upon me.

I was accordingly transferred to this corps and bid a farewell forever to my old comrades. I immediately went off with this (now my) captain and the other men drafted from our brigade, and joined the corps in an old meetinghouse at the Peekskill. It was after dark when we arrived there. I had now got among a new set, who were, to a man, entire strangers to me. I had, of course, to form new acquaintances, but I was not long in doing that. I had a pretty free use of my tongue, and was sometimes apt to use it when there was no occasion for it. However, I soon found myself at home with them. We were all young men and therefore easy to get acquainted.

I found nothing more here for belly timber than I had in the line, and got nothing to eat till the second day after I had joined the corps. We then drew, if I remember right, two days' rations of our good old diet, salt shad. We were on the green before the meetinghouse and there were several cows feeding about the place. I went into the house to get something to put my fish into, or some other business, and stayed longer than I intended, or rather ought to have done, for when I came out again, one of the cows was just finishing her meal on my shad; the last I saw of it was the tail of a fish sticking out of the side of her mouth. But I got something among the men, as poorly as they were off, to sustain nature till I could get more by some means or other. Such shifts were nothing strange to us.

This corps of Miners was reckoned an honorable one; it consisted of three companies. All the officers were required to be acquainted with the sciences, and it was desirable to have as intelligent young men as could be procured to compose it, although some of us fell considerably short of perfection. Agreeable to the arrangement between my former commander and my new captain, I was appointed a sergeant in this corps, which was as high an office as I ever obtained in the army, and I had some doubts in my own mind, at the time, whether I was altogether qualified for that. However, I was a sergeant and I think I *did* use my best abilities to perform the duties of the office according to my best knowledge and judgment.

Soon after I had joined this corps, the army moved down on the west side of the Hudson to Orange-town, commonly called by the inhabitants of those parts, Tappan. Just before arriving at our encamping ground, we halted in the road an hour or two. Some four or five of our men, knowing that the regiments to which they formerly belonged were near, slipped off for a few minutes to see their old messmates.

The Campaign of 1780

When we came to march again, they not having returned, I was ordered to remain with their arms and knapsacks till they came and then bring them on and join the corps again.

I waited an hour or two before they all returned. As soon as I had got them all together we set off, but the troops arriving and passing in almost every direction, I knew not where to go to find our corps. After much trouble and vexation (being constantly interrogated by the passing officers, who we were, and how we came to be behind our troops), I concluded, that as most or all the troops had passed us, to stay where I then was and wait the coming up of the baggage of our troops, thinking that the guard or drivers might have directions where to find them. Our baggage happening to be quite in the rear, while we were waiting we had an opportunity to see the baggage of the army pass. When that of the middle states passed us, it was truly amusing to see the number and habiliments of those attending it. Of all specimens of human beings, this group capped the whole. A caravan of wild beasts could bear no comparison with it. There was "Tag, Rag and Bobtail"; "some in rags and some in jags," but none "in velvet gowns." Some with two eyes, some with one, and some, I believe, with none at all. They "beggared all description."

I was glad to see the tail end of the train, and waited with impatience for the arrival of our baggage, which soon after made its appearance. But the men with the wagons knew no better than myself

137

where to go. We, however, proceeded and soon met one of the sergeants coming to conduct us to where our people were, which was at Dobbs Ferry, and about three miles from any part of the rest of the army. Most of the artillery belonging to the army was at the same place.

Here we lay till the close of the campaign.

I was about this time ordered to return up the river, in company with one of our lieutenants, after some clothing for our men. The lieutenant rode in company with an officer of the artillery, who was going that way upon business of his own, and I went on foot and started early in the morning with only my blanket and provisions (that is, if I had any).

I crossed King's Ferry and went on to the foot of the Highlands, where there was a commissary and wagoners, boatmen, &c. Here I again joined my lieutenant and obtained a ration or two of provisions, consisting of corned beef and hard bread, borrowed a pot, cooked my meat, ate my supper, turned in under an old wagon and slept soundly till about an hour before day, when the lieutenant called me up to go on to Newburgh, about twenty miles further up the river. He had procured a bateau and five or six men to convey us up and bring down the clothing which we were after. We had a mile or two to go to reach the boat, over ledges, through brush, and as dark as Egypt. We then proceeded to Newburgh, where we got our clothing. While I was packing it away in empty hogsheads, the lieutenant gave me a

hint to take care of my own interest. I accordingly picked from the best of each article what was allowed to each man and bundled them up by themselves. Afterwards, when a distribution was made, some of the sergeants were a little inclined to cavil with me for my partiality to myself. But the lieutenant interfered in my favor, telling them that I deserved the preference, as I had been at so much pains and trouble while they had remained at home at their ease.

We returned down the river on our way to camp until we came to where we took the boat, when I was set on shore to take the lieutenant's and the other officers' horses to King's Ferry, while the lieutenant went down in the boat. I took the horses and went on alone to the ferry.

I crossed the ferry in a large scow. There were ten or twelve head of cattle, besides my horses, in the boat. About midway of the river a cow jumped out and took her departure directly down the river. It being ebb tide and the water rapid, she was soon out of sight. There was not the least exertion made to save her. She was Continental property and *consequently* thought of but little *consequence*.

I landed and soon found my officer, who had arrived some time before me. He had got our baggage into a wagon, which had gone on, and he was waiting for me. We should have gone down to Dobbs Ferry with the boat, had it not been for the British brig *Vulture*, which was lying just below King's Ferry. There was a large number of wagons, teamsters and soldiers at the ferry. Everything destined to the army, coming down the river, was obliged to be landed here on account of the above-mentioned brig.

We went on and overtook the wagons. There were more than fifty wagons in company with us, bound to the army. We halted at night at a cluster of houses. The lieutenant took up his abode for the night in a farmer's house. I stayed out with the wagons. We started early next morning and arrived at Dobbs Ferry about noon.

We were frequently alarmed while lying at Dobbs Ferry. Being so few and at a distance from the main army, we had constantly to be on the lookout, but never happened to come in contact with the enemy, although they very frequently made us believe we should.

We lay at Dobbs Ferry till the latter part of the month of October, when we marched to West Point for winter quarters.

At the Peekskill we procured bateaux to convey ourselves and baggage up the river to the Point, where we arrived in safety and went into the old barracks, until new ones could be built for us, which we immediately commenced. We had to go six miles down the river, and there hew the timber, then carry it on our shoulders to the river, and then raft it to West Point. We, however, soon completed this part of the business ourselves, when the carpenters took it in hand, and by New Year's Day they were ready to receive us. Till then, we had been living in the old barracks, where there were rats enough, had they been men, to garrison twenty West Points.

Our barracks being completed, and we safely stowed away in them, I shall here conclude the campaign of 1780.

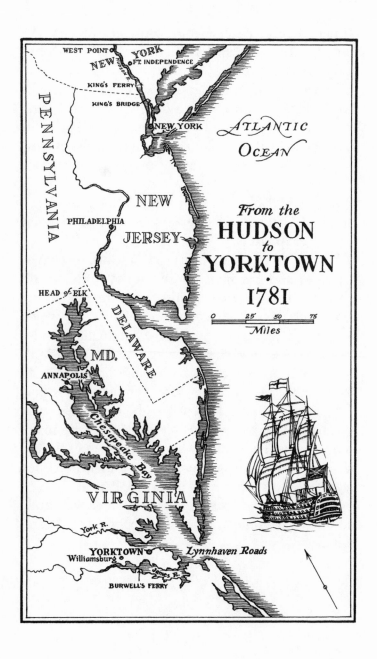

WEST POINT
NEW YORK
FT. INDEPENDENCE
KING'S FERRY
KING'S BRIDGE
NEW YORK
PENNSYLVANIA
NEW
JERSEY
PHILADELPHIA
ATLANTIC
OCEAN

From the
HUDSON
to
YORKTOWN
·
1781

0   25   50   75
Miles

HEAD of ELK
DELAWARE
MD.
ANNAPOLIS
Chesapeake Bay
VIRGINIA
York R.
YORKTOWN
Williamsburg
Lynnhaven Roads
James R.
BURWELL'S FERRY

VII
The Campaign of 1781

Back from furlough, Martin finds that his corps has marched for Virginia with General Lafayette. He follows on foot alone more than three hundred miles and overtakes it at Annapolis—just in time to sail back to West Point! The French, who have come to America's aid with armies and fleets, now join the Continentals on the Hudson River, and the combined forces move down close to the British at New York. Suddenly Washington marches them to Virginia to cooperate with the French fleet in an attempt to trap British General Cornwallis. By ship and foot, Martin's corps reaches Yorktown in Virginia, where he encounters General Washington, joins in the storming of the British fortifications, and sees the Redcoats lay down their arms.

Nothing material occurred to me till the month of February. About the twentieth of that month I took it into my head to apply to my captain for a recommendation to our colonel for a furlough, that I might once more visit my friends, for I saw no likelihood that the war would ever end. The captain told me that the colonel was about sending a noncommissioned officer into Connecticut after two men belonging to our corps who had been furloughed but had stayed beyond the time allowed them, and that he

143

would endeavor to have me sent on this business, and that after I had sent the delinquents to camp, I might tarry a space at home.

When I arrived at home I found that my good old grandmother was gone to her long home, and my grandsire gone forty miles back into the country, to his son's, and I never saw him afterwards. My sister was keeping the house, and I was glad to see her, as I had not seen her for several years. There was like- wise a neighbor's daughter there, who kept as much as she possibly could with my sister. Their company and conversation made up for the absence of my grandparents, it being a little more congenial to my age and feelings.

I stayed at home two or three days, to recruit after my journey, when a man belonging to our company, going home on furlough, called and informed me that one of the men I was after had arrived at camp, and as he should pass through the town where the other resided, he agreed to do my errand for me. With this arrangement I was much pleased, as it would save me about sixty miles travel in all, and I gave him a dollar to help him along, which was all the money I had. I had nothing now to do but to recreate myself, for, as the time of my return to the army was indefinitely set, I did not trouble myself about it.

I did, indeed, enjoy myself about ten days as agreeably as ever I did in the same space of time in my life; but I was loath to trespass upon my good colonel's indulgence, and therefore began to think

The Campaign of 1781

about my return. And as there was two men, one an old associate and the other a private citizen, who were going to camp, I thought, for company's sake, I would go with them. But I confess that I never left my home with so much regret before. I need not tell the reason; perhaps the reader can guess.

When I arrived within sight and hearing of the garrison of West Point, it again harrowed up my melancholy feelings that had, in a manner, subsided on my journey. But what added to my perturbation mostly was that I found our barracks entirely unoccupied, our men all gone, and not a soul could tell me where. What to do I knew not; I had a great mind to set off for home again, but at length concluded that I would try a little longer to find which way the men had gone. I therefore went to the issuing commissary of the garrison, and he soon informed me that they had gone to Virginia with General Lafayette. I was thunderstruck at this intelligence. The commissary, observing my chagrin, told me that my captain and eight or ten of our people were in the country, about twenty miles off, where they were undergoing the operation of the smallpox. The next day I went out to them and remained with them two or three days, but that would not do for me. I told the captain that I would go after the men. He said I might act my pleasure but that he should advise me to stay with him till he had got through with the smallpox and the other men that were with him had recovered, and then they should all go together. But that would not content me; I was as uneasy as a fish

145

out of the water. The captain then told me that if I was determined to follow the corps that my arms were with him and I might take them and go. I took them and went back to West Point, to the commissary, where I procured three or four rations of provisions and an order for five or six more, in case I could find any commissary on the way. The commissary filled my canteen with liquor, and thus equipped I set off on my journey alone, not expecting to find the men within less than four hundred miles.

I encountered nothing very material on my journey, except fatigue and some want, until I arrived at Annapolis, in Maryland. There I found what I had so long sought after, the Sappers and Miners. They were returning to West Point. They were on board vessels and were blocked in at Annapolis by some British ships at the mouth of the river. Shortly after I joined them, an opportunity offered and we escaped with our little fleet, by sweeping out in a dark night, and went up the bay.

We went directly on to West Point and took possession of our new barracks again and remained there till sometime in the month of May, when we, with the rest of the army in the Highlands, moved down and encamped at the Peekskill. We remained here awhile and then moved down near King's Bridge, fifteen miles from New York. A part of the army, under the command of General [Benjamin] Lincoln, fell down the river in bateaux and landed near old Fort Independence, where they were soon attacked by the enemy, when a smart skirmish ensued. Our corps, among others, immediately marched to reinforce General Lincoln, but the action ceased and the enemy had retired before we could arrive.

We lay on the ground we then occupied till after midnight, when we advanced further down towards Morrisania. At the dawn of day we were in close neighborhood with a British redoubt and saw a single horseman of the enemy reconnoitering us. We sent a platoon of men around a hill to cut off his retreat. But mistrusting our scheme, he kept off out of our reach, although he was seen near us the greater part of the day, "cutting his capers." As soon as it was fairly light we halted, and remained there all day and the night following.

The next morning we were joined by the French army from Rhode Island. Between us and the British redoubt there was a large deep gully. Our officers gave leave to as many as chose, of our men, to go over the gully and skirmish with the small parties of horsemen and footmen that kept patrolling from the redoubt to the gully, watching that none of us took shelter there to annoy them. Accordingly, a number of us kept disturbing their tranquillity all day.

Our people fired several shots from their fieldpieces at some boats crossing the water to the redoubt, but never fired a single shot at the redoubt, or they at us, although we were lying all day in open sight of each other and within half a mile distant. There seemed to be a tacit agreement between them not to injure one another.

We lay all night upon the ground which we had occupied during the day. I was exceedingly tired, not having had a wink of sleep the preceding night, and had been on my feet during the last twenty-four hours, and this night, to add to my comfort, I had to take charge of the quarter guard. I was allowed to get what rest I could consistently with our safety. I fixed my guard, placed two sentinels, and the remainder of us laid down.

Sometime in the night, the sentry by the guard stopped two or three officers who were going past us. The sentry called me up, and I took the strangers to our officers, where they went through an examination and were then permitted to pass on. I returned to my guard and lay down till called up again to relieve the sentinels. All this time I was as unconscious of what was passing as though nothing of the kind had happened, nor could I remember anything of the matter when told of it the next day, so completely was I worn down by fatigue.

We now fell back a few miles and encamped at a place called Philipse Manor. We then went to making preparations to lay siege to New York. We made fascines and gabions, the former, bundles of brush, and the latter are made in this manner, viz.—after setting sticks in the ground in a circle, about two feet or more in diameter, they are interwoven with small brush in form of a basket; they are then laid by for use in entrenching. Three or more rows of them are set down together (breaking joints), the trench is then dug behind and the dirt thrown into

148

them, which, when full, together with the trench, forms a complete breastwork. The word is pronounced *gab-beens*. The fascines (pronounced *fasheens*) are, as I said, bundles of brush bound snugly together, cut off straight at each end; they are of different lengths, from five to twelve feet. Their use is in building batteries and other temporary works.

We now expected soon to lay close siege to New York. Our Sappers and Miners were constantly employed with the engineers in front of the army, making preparations for the siege.

We remained at Philipse Manor till the last of July. The first of August, we all of a sudden marched from this ground and directed our course towards King's Ferry, near the Highlands, crossed the Hudson and lay there a few days, till the baggage, artillery, &c. had crossed, and then proceeded into New Jersey. We went down to Chatham, where were ovens built for the accommodation of the French troops. We then expected we were to attack New York in that quarter, but after staying here a day or two, we again moved off and arrived at Trenton by rapid marches. It was about sunset when we arrived here and instead of encamping for the night, as we expected, we were ordered immediately on board vessels then lying at the landing place, and a little after sunrise found ourselves at Philadelphia.

We Sappers and Miners stayed here some days, proving and packing off shells, shot, and other military stores. While we stayed here we drew a few

articles of clothing, consisting of a few tow shirts, some overalls and a few pairs of silk-and-oakum stockings. And here, or soon after, we each of us received a MONTH'S PAY, in specie, borrowed, as I was informed, by our French officers from the officers in the French army. This was the first that could be called money, which we had received as wages since the year '76, or that we ever did receive till the close of the war, or indeed, ever after, as wages.

When we had finished our business at Philadelphia, we (the Miners) left the city. A part of our men, with myself, went down the Delaware in a schooner which had her hold nearly full of gunpowder. Just after passing Mud Island, in the afternoon, we had a smart thundershower. I did not feel very agreeably, I confess, during its continuance, with such a quantity of powder under my feet. I was not quite sure that a stroke of the electric fluid might not compel me to leave the vessel sooner than I wished—but no accident happened, and we proceeded down the river to the mouth of Christiana Creek, up which we were bound.

We were compelled to anchor here on account of wind and tide. Here we passed an uneasy night from fear of British cruisers, several of which were in the bay. In the morning we got under way and proceeded up the creek fourteen miles, till the vessel grounded for lack of water. We then lightened her by taking out a part of her cargo, and when the tide came in we got up to the wharves and left her at the disposal of the artillerists.

We then crossed over land to the head of the Elk, or the head of Chesapeake Bay. Here we found a *large* fleet of *small* vessels waiting to convey us and other troops, stores, &c. down the bay. We soon embarked, that is, such of us as went by water, the greater part of the army having gone on by land.

We passed down the bay, making a grand appearance with our mosquito fleet, to Annapolis, which I had left about five months before for West Point. Here we stopped, fearing to proceed any further at present, not knowing exactly how matters were going on down the bay. A French cutter was dispatched to procure intelligence. She returned in the course of three or four days, bringing word that the passage was clear. We then proceeded and soon arrived at the mouth of James River [in Virginia] where were a number of armed French vessels and two or three fifty-gun ships. We passed in sight of the French fleet, then lying in Lynnhaven Bay; they resembled a swamp of dry pine trees. We had passed several of their men-of-war higher up the bay.

We were obliged to stay here a day or two on account of a severe northeast rainstorm. After the storm had ceased, we proceeded up the [James] River to a place called Burwell's Ferry [near Williamsburg], where the fleet all anchored. We landed the next day in the afternoon.

Soon after landing we marched to Williamsburg, where we joined General Lafayette, and very soon after, our whole army arriving, we prepared to move down and pay our old acquaintance, the British, at

The Campaign of 1781

Yorktown, a visit. I doubt not but their wish was not to have so many of us come at once, as their accommodations were rather scanty. They thought, "The fewer the better cheer." We thought, "The more the merrier." We had come a long way to see them and were unwilling to be put off with excuses. We thought the present time quite as convenient, at least for us, as any future time could be. We accordingly persisted, hoping that, as they pretended to be a very courtly people, they would have the politeness to come out and meet us, which would greatly shorten the time to be spent in the visit, and save themselves and us much labor and trouble. But they were too impolite at this time to do so.

We marched from Williamsburg the last of September. It was a warm day [the twenty-eighth]. When we had proceeded about halfway to Yorktown we halted and rested two or three hours. Being about to cook some victuals, I saw a fire which some of the Pennsylvania troops had kindled a short distance off. I went to get some fire while some of my messmates made other preparations. I had taken off my coat and unbuttoned my waistcoat, it being (as I said before) very warm. My pocketbook, containing about five dollars in money and some other articles, in all about seven dollars, was in my waistcoat pocket. When I came among the strangers they appeared to be uncommonly complaisant, asking many questions, helping me to fire, and chatting very familiarly. I took my fire and returned, but it was not long before I perceived that those kindhearted helpers had helped themselves to my pocketbook and its whole contents.

Here, or about this time, we had orders from the Commander in Chief that, in case the enemy should come out to meet us, we should exchange but one round with them and then decide the conflict with the bayonet, as they valued themselves at that instrument. The French forces could play their part at it, and the Americans were never backward at trying its virtue. The British, however, did not think fit at that time to give us an opportunity to soil our bayonets in their carcasses, but why they did not we could never conjecture. We as much expected it as we expected to find them there.

We went on and soon arrived and encamped in their neighborhood, without molestation. Our Miners lay about a mile and a half from their works, in open view of them. Here again we encountered our old associate, Hunger. Affairs, as they respected provisions, &c., were not yet regulated. No eatable stores had arrived, nor could we expect they should until we knew what reception the enemy would give us. We were, therefore, compelled to try our hands at foraging again. We, that is, our corps of Miners, were encamped near a large wood. There was a plenty of shoats all about this wood, fat and plump, weighing, generally, from fifty to a hundred pounds apiece. We soon found some of them and as no owner appeared to be at hand and the hogs not understanding our inquiries (if we made any) sufficiently to inform us to whom they belonged, we made free with some of them to satisfy the calls of nature till we could be better supplied.

We now began to make preparations for laying close siege to the enemy. We had holed him and nothing remained but to dig him out. Accordingly, after taking every precaution to prevent his escape, [we] settled our guards, provided fascines and gabions, made platforms for the batteries, to be laid down when needed, brought on our battering pieces, ammunition, &c. On the fifth of October we began to put our plans into execution.

One-third part of all the troops were to be employed in opening the trenches. A third part of our Sappers and Miners were ordered out this night to assist the engineers in laying out the works. It was a very dark and rainy night. However, we repaired to the place and began by following the engineers and laying laths of pine wood end-to-end upon the line marked out by the officers for the trenches. We had not proceeded far in the business before the engineers ordered us to desist and remain where we were and be sure not to straggle a foot from the spot while they were absent from us.

In a few minutes after their departure, there came a man alone to us, having on a surtout, as we conjectured, it being exceeding dark, and inquired for the engineers. We now began to be a little jealous for our safety, being alone and without arms, and within forty rods of the British trenches. The stranger inquired what troops we were, talked familiarly with us a few minutes, when, being informed which way

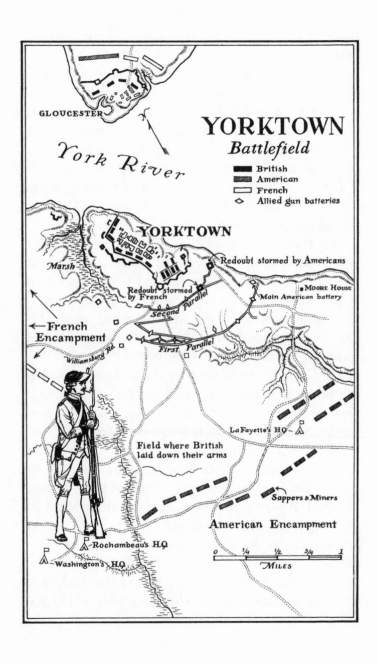

GLOUCESTER

York River

YORKTOWN
Battlefield

■ British
▨ American
▢ French
◇ Allied gun batteries

YORKTOWN

Marsh

Redoubt stormed by Americans

Redoubt stormed by French

Second Parallel

■ MOORE HOUSE
Main American battery

← French Encampment

First Parallel

Williamsburg Rd.

Field where British laid down their arms

LaFayette's H.Q.

Sappers & Miners

American Encampment

Rochambeau's H.Q.

Washington's H.Q.

0   1/4   1/2   3/4   1
MILES

the officers had gone, he went off in the same direction, after strictly charging us, in case we should be taken prisoners, not to discover to the enemy what troops we were. We were obliged to him for his kind advice, but we considered ourselves as standing in no great need of it, for we knew as well as he did that Sappers and Miners were allowed no quarter, at least, are entitled to none, by the laws of warfare, and of course should take care, if taken, not to betray our own secret.

In a short time the engineers returned and the afore-mentioned stranger with them. They discoursed together some time when, by the officers often calling him "Your Excellency," we discovered that it was General Washington. Had we dared, we might have cautioned him for exposing himself too carelessly to danger at such a time, and doubtless he would have taken it in good part if we had. But nothing ill happened to either him or ourselves.

It coming on to rain hard, we were ordered back to our tents, and nothing more was done that night. The next night, which was the sixth of October, the same men were ordered to the lines that had been there the night before. We this night completed laying out the works. The troops of the line were there ready with entrenching tools and began to entrench, after General Washington had struck a few blows with a pickax—a mere ceremony—that it might be said "General Washington with his own hands first broke ground at the siege of Yorktown."

The ground was sandy and soft, and the men employed that night eat no "idle bread" (and I question if they eat any other), so that by daylight they had covered themselves from danger from the enemy's shot, who, it appeared, never mistrusted that we were so near them the whole night, their attention being directed to another quarter. There was upon the right of their works a marsh. Our people had sent to the western side of this marsh a detachment to make a number of fires, by which (and our men often passing before the fires) the British were led to imagine that we were about some secret mischief there, and consequently directed their whole fire to that quarter, while we were entrenching literally under their noses.

As soon as it was day, they perceived their mistake and began to fire where they ought to have sooner. They brought out a fieldpiece or two and discharged several shots at the men who were at work erecting a bomb battery, but their shot had no effect and they soon gave it over. They had a large bulldog and every time they fired he would follow their shots across our trenches. Our officers wished to catch him and oblige him to carry a message from them into the town to his masters, but he looked too formidable for any of us to encounter.

I do not remember, exactly, the number of days we were employed before we got our batteries in readiness to open upon the enemy, but think it was not more than two or three. The French, who were upon our left, had completed their batteries a few hours before us, but were not allowed to discharge

their pieces till the American batteries were ready. Our commanding battery was on the near bank of the [York] river and contained ten heavy guns; the next was a bomb battery of three large mortars; and so on through the whole line. The whole number, American and French, was ninety-two cannon, mortars and howitzers. Our flagstaff was in the ten-gun battery, upon the right of the whole. I was in the trenches the day that the batteries were to be opened. All were upon the tiptoe of expectation and impatience to see the signal given to open the whole line of batteries, which was to be the hoisting of the American flag in the ten-gun battery.

About noon the much-wished-for signal went up. I confess I felt a secret pride swell my heart when I saw the "star-spangled banner" waving majestically in the very faces of our implacable adversaries. It appeared like an omen of success to our enterprise, and so it proved in reality. A simultaneous discharge of all the guns in the line followed, the French troops accompanying it with "Huzza for the Americans!"

It was said that the first shell sent from our batteries entered an elegant house formerly owned or occupied by the Secretary of State under the British government, and burst directly over a table surrounded by a large party of British officers at dinner, killing and wounding a number of them. This was a warm day to the British.

The siege was carried on warmly for several days, when most of the guns in the enemy's works were silenced. We now began our second parallel, about halfway between our works and theirs. There were two strong redoubts held by the British, on their left. It was necessary for us to possess those redoubts before we could complete our trenches. One afternoon, I, with the rest of our corps, was ordered to the lines. I mistrusted something extraordinary was going forward, but what I could not easily conjecture.

We arrived at the trenches a little before sunset [October 14]. I saw several officers fixing bayonets on long staves. I then concluded we were about to make a general assault upon the enemy's works, but before dark I was informed of the whole plan, which was to storm the redoubts, the one by the Americans and the other by the French.

The Sappers and Miners were furnished with axes and were to proceed in front and cut a passage for the troops through the abatis, which are composed of the tops of trees, the small branches cut off with a slanting stroke which renders them as sharp as spikes. These trees are then laid at a small distance from the trench or ditch, pointing outwards, and the butts fastened to the ground in such a manner that they cannot be removed by those on the outside of them. It is almost impossible to get through them. Through these we were to cut a passage before we or the other assailants could enter.

At dark the detachment was formed and advanced beyond the trenches and lay down on the ground to await the signal for advancing to the attack, which was to be three shells from a certain battery near where we were lying. All the batteries in our line were silent, and we lay anxiously waiting for the signal. The two brilliant planets, Jupiter and Venus, were in close contact in the western hemisphere, the same direction that the signal was to be made in. When I happened to cast my eyes to that quarter, which was often, and I caught a glance of them, I was ready to spring on my feet, thinking they were the signal for starting. Our watchword was "Rochambeau," the commander of the French forces' name, a good watchword, for being pronounced *Rosham-bow*, it sounded, when pronounced quick, like *rush-on-boys*.

We had not lain here long before the expected signal was given, for us and the French, who were to storm the other redoubt, by the three shells with their fiery trains mounting the air in quick succession. The word *up, up*, was then reiterated through the detachment. We immediately moved silently on toward the redoubt we were to attack, with unloaded muskets. Just as we arrived at the abatis, the enemy discovered us and directly opened a sharp fire upon us. We were now at a place where many of our large shells had burst in the ground, making holes sufficient to bury an ox in. The men, having their eyes fixed upon what was transacting before them, were every now and then falling into these holes. I thought the British were killing us off at a great rate. At length, one of the holes happening to pick me up, I found out the mystery of the huge slaughter.

As soon as the firing began, our people began to

cry, "The fort's our own!" and it was "Rush on, boys." The Sappers and Miners soon cleared a passage for the infantry, who entered it rapidly. Our Miners were ordered not to enter the fort, but there was no stopping them. "We will go," said they. "Then go to the d——l," said the commanding officer of our corps, "if you will."

I could not pass at the entrance we had made, it was so crowded. I therefore forced a passage at a place where I saw our shot had cut away some of the abatis. Several others entered at the same place. While passing, a man at my side received a ball in his head and fell under my feet, crying out bitterly. While crossing the trench, the enemy threw hand grenades into it. They were so thick that I at first thought them cartridge papers on fire, but was soon undeceived by their cracking. As I mounted the breastwork, I met an old associate hitching himself down into the trench. I knew him by the light of the enemy's musketry, it was so vivid.

The fort was taken and all quiet in a very short time. Immediately after the firing ceased, I went out to see what had become of my wounded friend and the other that fell in the passage. They were both dead. In the heat of the action I saw a British soldier jump over the walls of the fort next the river and go down the bank, which was almost perpendicular and twenty or thirty feet high. When he came to the beach he made off for the town, and if he did not make good use of his legs I never saw a man that did.

All that were in the action of storming the redoubt

were exempted from further duty that night. We laid down upon the ground and rested the remainder of the night—as well as a constant discharge of grape and canister shot would permit us to do—while those who were on duty for the day completed the second parallel by including the captured redoubts within it. We returned to camp early in the morning, all safe and sound, except one of our lieutenants, who had received a slight wound on the top of the shoulder by a musket shot. Seven or eight men belonging to the infantry were killed, and a number wounded.

Our duty was hazardous but not very hard. We were on duty in the trenches twenty-four hours, and forty-eight hours in camp. The invalids did the camp duty, and we had nothing else to do but to attend morning and evening roll calls and recreate ourselves as we pleased the rest of the time, till we were called upon to take our turns on duty in the trenches again. The greatest inconvenience we felt was the want of good water, there being none near our camp but nasty frog ponds where all the horses in the neighborhood were watered, and we were forced to wade through the water in the skirts of the ponds, thick with mud and filth, to get at water in any wise fit for use, and that full of frogs. All the springs about the country, although they looked well, tasted like water that had been standing in iron or copper vessels.

I was one day rambling alone in the woods when I came across a small brook of very good water, about a mile from our tents. We used this water daily to drink or we should have suffered. But it was "the fortune of war."

After we had finished our second line of trenches there was but little firing on either side. After Lord Cornwallis had failed to get off, upon the seventeenth day of October (a rather unlucky day for the British) he requested a cessation of hostilities for, I think, twenty-four hours, when commissioners from both armies met at a house between the lines to agree upon articles of capitulation. We waited with anxiety the termination of the armistice and as the time drew nearer our anxiety increased. The time at length arrived—it passed, and all remained quiet. And now we concluded that we had obtained what we had taken so much pains for, for which we had encountered so many dangers, and had so anxiously wished. Before night we were informed that the British had surrendered and that the siege was ended.

The next day we were ordered to put ourselves in as good order as our circumstances would admit, to see the British army march out and stack their arms. The trenches, where they crossed the road leading to the town, were leveled and all things put in order for this grand exhibition. After breakfast, on the nineteenth, we were marched onto the ground and paraded on the right-hand side of the road, and the French forces on the left. We waited two or three hours before the British made their appearance. They were not always so dilatory, but they were compelled at last, by necessity, to appear, all armed, with bayonets fixed, drums beating, and faces lengthening. They were led by General [Charles] O'Hara, with the American General Lincoln on his right, the Americans and French beating a march as they passed out between them. It was a noble sight to us, and the more so, as it seemed to promise a speedy conclusion to the contest.

The British did not make so good an appearance as the German forces, but there was certainly some allowance to be made in their favor. The English felt their honor wounded, the Germans did not greatly care whose hands they were in. The British paid the Americans, seemingly, but little attention as they passed them, but they eyed the French with considerable malice. They marched to the place appointed and stacked their arms. They then returned to the town in the same manner they had marched out, except being divested of their arms. After the prisoners were marched off into the country, our army separated, the French remaining where they then were and the Americans marching for the Hudson.

Editor's Afterword

Washington's victory over Cornwallis did not instantly end the war. Other British armies still held New York, Charleston and Savannah. King George III was not yet willing to admit defeat. So the American War for Independence dragged on for seventeen months more. While there was no more major fighting in America, Washington felt obliged to keep his armies ready in the field. It was a dull time, but it was a hard time for such war-weary veterans as Joseph Martin, who were confident now of final victory and eager to be done with the service and get home.

Following the surrender of Cornwallis, the main Continental Army returned to the banks of the Hudson River. Martin marched north with his corps of Sappers and Miners into New Jersey for the winter. In the spring of 1782, the corps went to West Point. In summer it moved to Constitution Island in the Hudson to repair fortifications. There, one day, some of the Sappers and Miners decided to play a reckless prank. Martin related it this way:

"Our captain had pitched his marquee in an old gravel pit, at some distance from the tents of the men. One day, two or three of our young hotheads told me that they and some others of the men, whom

167

they mentioned, were about to have some fun with 'the old man,' as they generally called the captain. I inquired what their plans were, and they informed me that they had put some powder into a canteen and were going to give him a bit of a hoist. I asked them to let me see their apparatus before they put their project in execution. Accordingly, they soon after showed me a wooden canteen with more, as I judged, than three pounds of gunpowder in it, with a stopper of touchwood for a fuse affixed to it, all, they said, in prime order. I told them they were crazy, that the powder they had in the canteen would 'hoist' him out of time, but they insisted upon proceeding. It would only frighten him, they said, and that was all they wished to do—it would make him a little more complaisant. I then told them that if they persisted in their determination and would not promise me on the spot to give up their scheme, I would that instant go to the captain and lay the whole affair before him. At length, after endeavoring without effect to obtain my consent to try a little under his berth, they concluded to give up the affair altogether, and thus, I verily believe, I saved the old man's life, although I do not think that they meant anything more than to frighten him."

Before the weather turned cold, the troops at Constitution Island built "a new range of barracks and elegant ones, too." Into them they moved when the snow came. And in them Martin rounded out his seventh year in the Continental Army.

That winter was not, in Martin's words, "over

gentle." Much of the time he served on guard duty. The island was hilly and windblown, and, said he, it would "make a sentry shake his ears" to stand two hours in the snow.

Here Martin "suffered again for eatables" and lived half the winter "upon tripe and cowheels and the other half upon what I could get." But for him and his comrades hope that the war was nearly over "buoyed us up under many difficulties."

At West Point each spring a massive iron chain with links two feet long that weighed 180 pounds apiece was strung across the Hudson to prevent enemy vessels from sailing up the river. The soldiers called it General Washington's watch chain. Each autumn, when military activities ceased for the winter (as they did in the eighteenth century), the chain was hauled up for repairs and storage. In the spring of 1783, the garrisons around West Point were full of rumors that the chain would not be put into the river again and rumors that it would. The soldiers felt that whether it was put down or not would reveal whether the army high command expected the war to continue. All spring one rumor chased another. Then, said Martin:

"At length the eleventh day of June, 1783, arrived. 'The old man,' our captain, came into our room, with his hands full of papers, and first ordered us to empty all our cartridge boxes upon the floor (this was the last order he ever gave us) and then told us that if we needed them we might take some of them again. They were all immediately gathered up and returned

169

to our boxes. Government had given us our arms and we considered the ammunition as belonging to them, and he had neither right nor orders to take them from us. He then handed us our discharges, or rather furloughs, for they were in appearance no other than furloughs, permission to return home, but to return to the army again if required. This was policy in government; to discharge us absolutely in our present pitiful, forlorn condition, it was feared, might cause some difficulties which might be too hard for government to get easily over.

"The powder in our cartridges was soon burnt. Some saluted the officers with large charges; others only squibbed them, just as each one's mind was affected toward them. Our 'old man' had a number of these last-mentioned symbols of honor and affection presented him. Some of the men were not half so liberal in the use of powder as they were when they would have given him a canteenful at once.

"I confess, after all, that my anticipation of the happiness I should experience upon such a day as this was not realized; I can assure the reader that there was as much sorrow as joy transfused on the occasion. We had lived together as a family of brothers for several years, setting aside some little family squabbles like most other families, had shared with each other the hardships, dangers, and sufferings incident to a soldier's life; had sympathized with each other in trouble and sickness; had assisted in bearing each other's burdens or strove to make them lighter by council and advice; had endeavored to

171

conceal each other's faults or make them appear in as good a light as they would bear. In short, the soldiers, each in his particular circle of acquaintance, were as strict a band of brotherhood as Masons and, I believe, as faithful to each other. And now we were to be, the greater part of us, parted forever, as unconditionally separated as though the grave lay between us. I question if there was a corps in the army that parted with more regret than ours did, the New Englanders in particular. Ah! it was a serious time."

Some of the soldiers went home, Martin said, "the same day their fetters were knocked off" assuming that in time their pay would be sent to them. But Martin was loath to leave without money in hand. So he stayed on, serving a short enlistment for another man until final pay certificates were issued. He then bought some "decent clothing" and struck out through the Hudson Highlands. Accidentally he ran into a friend with whom he tarried for a while. Then, as winter was approaching, he agreed to teach school among the Dutch until spring.

When 1784 rolled around, Joseph Martin bade his pupils and friends farewell and, as he said, "set my face to the eastward and made no material halt till I arrived in the state of Maine." There he remained ever afterward, living a long, useful and happy life. And there, in a big frame house in the town of Prospect, on Penobscot Bay, he set down what you have read, his recollections of the adventures, dangers, and sufferings of a youthful, valiant, and devoted Continental soldier.

Illustrated Glossary

of

18th Century Military Terms

Glossary of Military Terms

ABATIS: A defense made by placing felled trees so that their branches turned toward the enemy. The trunks were sometimes buried in the ground and the boughs interwoven, making the abatis especially difficult to penetrate. The branches often were sharpened.

ACCOUTERMENTS: Such items carried by the soldier as his bayonet belt, pouch, and cartridge box.

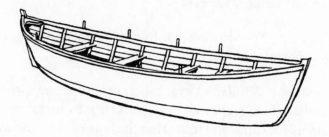

BATEAU: A long, light flat-bottomed boat, tapering at both ends, rowed or poled in shallow waters.

BATTERY: Any place where cannon were mounted.

BILLET: To house soldiers in private houses. Also the place where they were thus housed.

BOMB: A hollow iron ball filled with gunpowder and equipped with a fuse which ignited when the bomb was fired from a mortar.

BOMB BATTERY: A battery whose guns were mortars. *See* Mortar.

BROTHER JONATHAN: First used by the British as a scornful nickname for a typical New Englander, Yankee, or American. Eventually it became a term for the American people as a whole and for the United States. After the Revolution, the Americans adopted the nickname with pride.

CALIBER: The diameter of the inside of a cannon or gun barrel.

CANISTER: Similar to grapeshot. Ironshot somewhat smaller than grapeshot was packed into metal containers (or canisters) that fitted the bore of the cannon. When fired the canister exploded, scattering the shot.

CANTONMENT: The place of encampment of troops

for an extended stay during a campaign or while in winter quarters. Also used to refer to temporary buildings or shelters for housing troops.

CHEVAUX-DE-FRISE: In naval use, a device for blocking passage in a river or harbor. Usually it was constructed by embedding iron-pointed wooden beams into large crate-like structures which were loaded with stones and sunk in the river or harbor. The beams sloped up within a few feet of the surface to spear or rip the hulls of advancing vessels.

COMMISSARY: An officer in charge of a special service. There were commissaries for various departments of the army, such as commissary of provisions, commissary of clothing, etc.

CONTINENTALS: The "regular" soldiers of the American army.

FASCINES: Long bundles of brushwood or small tree branches bound together and used for filling ditches and as bases for earthworks.

FIELDPIECE: A light-weight cannon, mounted on a two-wheel carriage, for use on a field of battle.

FORAGE: Hay, straw and oats for feeding horses and cattle. Also, to search for such food.

GABION: A cylindrical basket made of interwoven twigs, open at both ends, to be filled with earth and used in making fortifications and gun batteries.

GRAPESHOT: Solid, small round shot. A wooden disk from whose center protruded a short wooden rod was set in a cloth bag and the bag filled with fifty or sixty grapeshot. The bag was then tightly laced with cord. When the load was fired from a cannon, the bag burned away and the shot scattered. Grapeshot was used at relatively short range against massed troops and cavalry.

GRASSHOPPER: A small cannon on a wheeled carriage with shafts for hitching to a single horse.

GRENADE: A small, hollow ball or shell filled with fine powder and fired by a fuse. The grenade was hand-thrown.

HESSIANS: Soldiers from Hesse-Cassel, Germany, who were hired out by their prince to the British to fight in America. The idea that they were "bought" soldiers, fighting without conviction, was repugnant to most Americans. Soldiers from other states in Germany also served with the British, but they were all commonly called Hessians by the Americans.

HOWITZER: A short cannon, between a mortar and a fieldpiece in weight and character, mounted on a wheeled carriage, and used to throw a heavy shell at a high angle of elevation and farther than a mortar.

INVALIDS: Soldiers disabled for field service but capable of carrying on camp duties.

LANGRAGE: Similar to grapeshot, originally used at sea to destroy ships' rigging and sails. Bolts, nails, and other scrap metal were packed into a can which burst when fired from a cannon. Often the scrap metal was loaded loose.

LEVIES: Volunteer state troops raised as reinforcements for the army, usually for a limited time.

LIGHT INFANTRY: A special corps of young officers and men drawn from the regular regiments. They had to be agile, rugged and trustworthy, and were used for special and difficult missions and for the vanguard of the army.

MAN, or TO MAN THE WORKS: To post troops on the lines or works ready for defense.

MANUAL EXERCISE: The exercise of the musket, or practice in loading and firing, without powder and ball. The Manual of Arms as introduced into the Continental Army by Baron Frederick von Steuben at Valley Forge in early 1778 is illustrated on page 78 of the text.

MARQUEE: A large field tent used by officers, sometimes with an awning projecting over the entrance.

MATCH: A wick of rope chemically treated, in a tin tube, used to touch off muzzle-loaded artillery, much as a fuse ignited a shell.

MILITIA: Local bodies of citizen soldiers. In colonial America all able-bodied men between sixteen and sixty-five (except certain exempts) were required to perform military exercises a certain number of days a year and were subject to military call. Usually they served near home on temporary duty and resented being called to distant fields. Less well trained than the regular army, they generally proved less steady and dependable in camp and on the battle field.

MINE: A passage dug under the wall or rampart of a fortification for the purpose of blowing it up with gunpowder.

MORTAR: A short, heavy cannon for throwing bombs at a high angle to reach targets behind obstructions such as fortress walls. In contrast to the solid shot of cannon, the mortar's bomb arched through the air and exploded just above or among troops or inside fortifications.

MOSQUITO FLEET: A fleet of small vessels associated in some way, as the smaller coasting vessels of one port or the torpedo boats of a navy.

MUSTER: A review of troops to see if their arms are complete and in good order.

PALISADO: A palisade or a protective wall of vertical, pointed tree-trunks or similar timbers.

PARALLEL: A siege line (deep trenches interspersed with batteries), usually parallel to the face of the fortification being besieged.

PLATFORM: A bed of wood in a battery upon which the cannon stood. The platform was usually raised slightly at the rear to prevent guns from recoiling too far.

PRIVATEER: An armed private vessel granted the right by a government to cruise against the commercial or war vessels of an enemy.

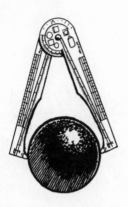

PROVE: To test weapons and ammunition for imperfections. A shell was proved by plugging the fuse hole and immersing it in water. If the water bubbled, the shell had a crack or hole in it and was rejected. A perfect shell was packed with powder and a fuse driven into it. Solid shot was proved to determine that it was perfectly round and its diameter was the right size for the cannon for which it was intended. Measuring was done with a pair of gunner's calipers or gages.

QUARTER: Mercy or life granted an enemy vanquished in battle or who had surrendered. Sappers and Miners seldom were granted quarter when captured.

QUARTER GUARD: A small guard placed about eighty paces in front of each battalion in a camp. Quarter guards were more for preserving the peace and quiet within the regiments than for security against an enemy.

REDOUBT: A small, enclosed fortification located so as to defend passes, hilltops, or the approaches to a main fortification.

REGULARS: Soldiers of a regular, or standing, army of a nation. Used in the Revolution to designate British troops. American "regulars" were called Continentals.

ROUND (*in firing*): A single, general discharge of cannon or of musketry.

SAP: A covered trench or tunnel for approaching or undermining a fortification.

184

Glossary of Military Terms

SAPPERS AND MINERS: A corps of men who worked with saps and mines. They also laid out and fortified camps, opened and repaired roads in advance of the army, reconnoitered, and performed other special tasks.

SAWNEY: A nickname for a Scotsman or for the Scots.

SQUIB: To fire a musket charged with loose powder but without ball or wadding to give it pressure. Squibbing produced an unpleasant sound and was a gesture of disapproval or insult when compared to the full salute of a charged musket.

Index

Abatis, 161, 162, 163
Accouterments, 24
Advance parties, duties of, 53-54
Amusements: backgammon, 55; rolling wagon wheels, 101, 108-110; plugging shells, 101, 108; "hoisting" the captain, 167-168
Annapolis, Md., 143, 146, 152

Barren Hill, Pa., 83, 85, 86
Basking Ridge, N.J., 112, 125
Bedford, N.Y., 98, 100
Bethlehem, Pa., 56
Bomb batteries, 61, 158, 160
Boston, Mass., 15, 17
Boston Tea Party, 16
Bristol, Pa., 69
Brooklyn, N.Y., 27
"Brother Jonathan," 46
Burlington, N.J., 69
Burwell's Ferry (James River), 152
Butler, Col. Richard, 97

Canada, 49
Canister, 28, 164

Cannonballs, caught by soldiers, 64
Chain, across Hudson, 169
Charleston, S.C., 167
Chatham, N.J., 149
Chesapeake Bay, 152
Chestnut Hill, Pa., 70, 71
Chevaux-de-frise, 64
Christiana Creek, 151
Christmas, 74, 80, 100
Cilly, Col. Joseph, 93
Concord, Mass., 9, 15
Congress, 71
Connecticut, 15, 21, 47, 98, 100, 101, 143
Connecticut troops, 51, 59, 66, 92, 93, 95, 98, 100, 110, 121, 131, 133
Constitution Island (Hudson River), 167, 168
Cooking utensils, 42-43, 57
Cornwallis, Lord, 9, 143, 165, 167
Coryell's Ferry (Delaware River), 86

Danbury, Conn., 51, 100
Delaware River, 49, 59, 60, 69, 86, 151

187

Index

North (or Hudson) River, 40, 132
Norwalk, Conn., 47, 110

O'Hara, Gen. Charles, 166
Old Orchard, N.Y., 51
Orangetown, N.Y., 135
Ovens, for French troops, 149

Palisadoes, 60, 62, 65
Parallels (trenches), 160
Peekskill, N.Y., 51, 54, 108, 111-112, 134, 141, 146
Pennsylvania, 12, 56
Pennsylvania troops, 97, 129, 130, 153
Penobscot Bay & River, 11, 172
Philadelphia, Pa., 49, 57, 58, 59, 70, 77, 83, 85, 86, 149, 151
Philipse Manor, N.Y., 48 148, 149
Phoenix (British ship), 35
Pitcher, Molly, 79, 95-96
Planets (Jupiter & Venus), 162
Princeton, N.J., 49, 86, 87
Privateers, 22
Prospect, Maine, 11, 172
Proving of shells, 149

Quarter (mercy), 157

Rangers, 39
Red Bank, N.J., 68
Redding, Conn., 100
Rhode Island, 147
Rhode Island troops, 88-89, 93

Robinson's farm, 112
"Rochambeau" (watchword), 162

Sappers and Miners, 118, 133-135, 146, 149, 151, 154, 155, 157, 161, 163, 167
Savannah, Ga., 167
"Sawney," 95
Schuylkill River, 71, 84, 85, 86
Scotch troops, 95
Smallpox, inoculation for, 49, 51-53, 82, 145
Spies, British, 133
Springfield, N.J., 121, 132
Squibbing, 171
Stamp Act, 16
Staten Island expedition, 118-119, 121, 122
Steuben, Baron von, 79, 83, 132
Stewart, Col. Walter, 130, 131
Stony Point, N.Y., 108, 110, 111

Tappan, N.Y., 135
Tarrytown, N.Y., 96
Thanksgiving, 71-74
Throg's Neck, or Point, 42
Tories, 21, 47, 54, 119
Trenton, N.J., 49, 86, 149
Tryon, Gov. William, 110
Turtle Bay (New York), 32

Valentine's Hill (N.Y.), 42
Valley Forge, Pa., 9, 49, 74, 75
Varnum, General, 93

Index

About the Editor

George F. Scheer's interest in writing about the American Revolution began in the sixth grade of William Fox elementary school in Richmond, Virginia, his native town, when his teacher assigned an essay on Washington's Christmas Night crossing of the Delaware. In his father's library he found an account of that surprise attack on Trenton written by one of Washington's staff officers, who described the scenes he himself witnessed on the storm-swept river, along the icy roads, and in the embattled streets of the town. This vivid, first-hand narrative did more to make that march real for that eleven-year-old boy of Richmond than anything he could find in the more formal histories written years after the event.

From that day to this, Mr. Scheer has sought eye-witness accounts of the American past. His boyhood discovery of the reality and excitement of personal narratives led him, in time, to write (with Hugh F. Rankin) *Rebels and Redcoats,* a major history of the war of the Revolution told largely in the words of participants. Later he became General Editor of the Meridian Documents of American History series, a multi-volume series of documentary histories, and editor of the unabridged autobiography of Joseph Plumb Martin, published under the title, *Private Yankee Doodle.* He has contributed articles to numerous newspapers and periodicals. In recognition of his contributions to military history he was made a Fellow of The Company of Military Historians. He is also a member of the Society of American Historians.

Mr. Scheer attended the University of Richmond and now lives in Chapel Hill, North Carolina.